The best got smaller...

Apple has made the iPad the best value it's ever been with the release of the iPad mini. Just because it's shrunk, though, that doesn't mean it's not still power-packed...

When Apple first released the original iPad in April 2010, there were many who were quick to rush in with their criticisms. Surely this was Apple just cashing in. It was a just bigger iPod Touch or iPhone. Who on earth would want to use one? Isn't a laptop a better bet?

It's fair to say that just a few years later those questions have been resolutely answered. By the end of 2012, sales of the iPad had crossed 100 millions, and it's since become a standard for tablet computing the world over. The iPad is now used for everything from business to gaming, and education to music. It's been a phenomenal success, and no one can deny that.

The advent of the iPad mini does two things. Firstly, it shrinks down the size of the iPad to a device that now fits comfortably in a coat pocket. Secondly, it brings the product down to a cheaper price as well. Incredibly, it does this without compromising on the power and functionality that has made the iPad the success it's been to date.

For such a complex product, though, the iPad mini isn't shipped with a manual. As such, while it's mostly easy to use and intuitive to get around, there are lots of added features that require a bit of help to get the most out of them. That's where we come in. Across these 180-pages we've put together a starting point for using and getting the most out of an iPad mini, with clear tutorials and no shortage of app recommendations to get you on your way.

There's a lot to talk about and get through, so we'll stop chatting and get down to business. Hopefully, by the time you get to the end of this guide, you'll have uncovered the many, many hidden secrets of Apple's latest version of its world-conquering tablet...

Contents

INTRODUCING
4G Technology **12**

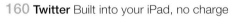

Your iPad mini And...
You

Before you can get the most out of the iPad mini, there are quite a few basics to get through. As such, we're going to use this chapter to go through a few things that you may already know and a few things that you might not.

It's certainly a device that's come a long, long way. Compared to the very first iPad that was released, the iPad mini is a far more powerful and capable beast, all the more impressive given its lower footprint. It's faster too, and it has very, very impressive battery life. It's the kind of battery life that asks some questions of its growing number of rivals too, who are struggling to match it.

After all, one of the reasons that Apple released the iPad mini in the first place was growing competition from smaller, 7" tablet devices - the Google Nexus 7, for instance, or the Amazon Kindle Fire, both of which are hardly shabby. Now, the iPad mini has firmly put them both in their place.

For the purposes of this chapter, we're going to explain why and how. We're going to take a look through what the iPad mini is and where it's come from. We'll look at how it works and compare it to its bigger brother, the iPad.

This is also where we're also going to take you through two areas that can really help you get the most out of your iPad mini: iOS 6 and iCloud.

iOS 6 is the operating system that underpins every app that the iPad mini runs, and we're going to show you how to get the most out of it. Furthermore, the iCloud system can be a real life saver. If you use iCloud, then you can access your content from different devices in different places, and it's really not very tricky to set up.

So let's begin, and give you a flavour of just what your iPad mini can do...

The iPad mini
An In-Depth Look

The iPad mini is the smallest iPad to date, but Apple's ensured it's still packed with an awful lot for your money...

For a long time, it seemed as though Apple wasn't interested in making a smaller version of its world-conquering iPad tablet. Rivals such as Amazon (with its Kindle Fire) and Google (with its Nexus 7) were instead taking advantage of the gap that Apple had left behind, offering smaller, more portable devices than Apple's physically larger iPad range of tablet computers.

Of course, it's folly, as many have found before, to second-guess just what Apple is up to, and in October of 2012, after much speculation, it finally took the wraps off the iPad mini, launching it just a few weeks later. With a screen size that's two inches smaller than that of the iPad, and a lower price to go with it, it's instantly managed to open up the world of the iPad to many who previously wanted something either more portable or less expensive (or both, of course).

To Apple's credit, the iPad mini doesn't cut out the functionality that we've come to expect from the iPad. In fact, apart from the physical footprint of the device, its capabilities are identical to the best-selling iPad 2. It would be wrong to think of the iPad mini therefore as a shrunken iPad. Apple has managed to pack in a good deal more than you may have initially expected.

The initial announcement introduced - as is becoming the norm for Apple - three different models of iPad mini, with 16GB, 32GB and 64GB storage capacities, and varying prices to match. Furthermore, a few weeks after the Wi-Fi-only iPad minis were introduced, Apple completed the line-up with 3G and 4G compatible versions too (again in three different storage flavours).

Whichever flavour you opt for, the iPad mini is a very light device, weighing in at just 308g. That's over 50% lighter than the iPad, and you can tell that from pretty much the minute you pick it up. Furthermore, it's also more than 20% thinner. Apple boasts that the iPad mini is pencil thin, and it's good on its claims. It still finds the space to include a front and back camera, a powerful A5 processor and room for an abundance of apps. It's just managed to pack them into a smaller device than it's managed before

Let's take a look at it all in a bit more detail...

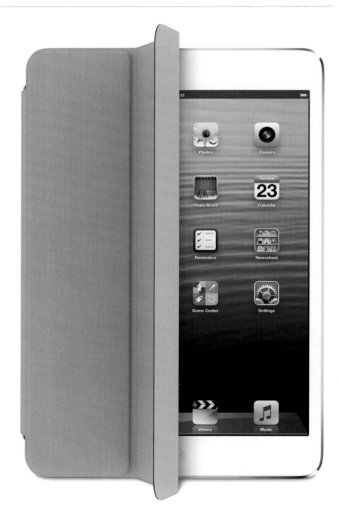

Screen Display

In spite of being the iPad with the smallest screen, Apple has included technologies that offset any problems that come with that. The screen measures 7.9 inches across, and the resolution is 1024 x 728. Furthermore, the pixel density is excellent, at 163 pixels per inch, compared to 132 on the iPad 2. Basically, that means it's possible to fit more images, more clearly on the screen.

Processing Power

The processor that sits at the heart of the iPad mini is the same one that's been powering the iPad 2 and third-generation iPad with no complaints. It's an ARM Cortex-A9 CPU running at 1GHz. Granted, this won't mean much to the majority of people and nor should it. The crucial factor here is that Apple has managed to put a powerful processor into its iPads, which doesn't eat up too much power. Furthermore, it's a dual-core processor. The advantage there, simply, is that the CPU can do two lots of work at the same time, which in turn improves performance.

Storage Space

As with the previous iPads, the iPad mini has been released in three distinct storage flavours: 16GB, 32GB and 64GB. The price varies notably between the three. The storage itself is handled by on-board flash memory, which again is power efficient. What's worth bearing in mind here is that if you're looking to download lots of movies and music, for example, to your iPad mini, that's just the kind of content that eats up storage space extremely quickly. Sadly, Apple's pricing for higher storage models seems a little heavy, but if you're after more space in your iPad mini, there's not too much you can do about it.

Battery Power

Not for the first time, the stats provided by Apple for the iPad mini seem like a mixture of fact and fiction – standby time still clocks in at a whole month, with ten hours of either Internet browsing via Wi-Fi (less through 3G or 4G) or video viewing on a single charge. Speaking from our own experience with our iPad, though, the actual time depends on how many Push notifications you have set up (the amount of apps you have trying to talk to your iPad via a Wi-Fi or 3G/4G signal). We like to think of ourselves as average users of things like social networking, email and text, but we still find ourselves charging our iPads every two to three days...

Software Support

Apple provides an abundance of useful tools built into the iPad mini, all centred around its iOS 6 operating system. Also built into modern iPads is Apple's iCloud service, as well as FaceTime communication software, Maps, photo and video tools, the Safari web browser and Newsstand. Dictation is now also supported as standard, as is the Siri voice-activated personal assistant, which truthfully seems better suited to iPhones than iPads.

Miscellaneous Facts

● The screen of the iPad mini is 7.9 inches, which makes it, ironically, the largest of the smaller tablets that Apple is competing with. Rival devices such as the aforementioned Kindle Fire and Nexus 7 have 7" screens, and are slightly smaller as a result. Not by much, though.

● The iPad mini comes with a different connector to most iPads. It's called the Lightning connector, and one advantage is that it's not possible to plug it in the wrong way round. The downside, though, is that existing iPad accessories that rely on a power connector are no longer compatible. Apple intends to use this new Lightning connector on its devices going forward.

● To give a bit more of a personal touch, Apple allows you to personalise your iPad mini when you order it from the Apple Store by having it engraved.

iPad mini

The iPad (4th Generation)
An In-Depth Look

Alongside the iPad mini, Apple also launched a new generation of iPad. Let's take a look at it...

In October 2012, Apple, not for the first time, attracted a fair amount of criticism. As expected, it had announced the launch of the iPad mini, but what took people by surprise was that it coupled it with the announcement of a fourth-generation release for its larger iPad line.

The reason this proved to be such a surprise was that the third-generation iPad has only been launched in March 2012, and that left many feeling let down, having been used to annual refreshes up until that point. Releasing a better version of the iPad just eight months after the previous one left some with a raw taste (although there had been complaints that the third-generation iPad wasn't a big enough jump over the iPad 2 as well).

It perhaps goes without saying that the fourth-generation iPad is Apple's most powerful tablet computer to date. And while there was a short gap between releases, there were some notable differences that have gone down really rather well.

Apple's most trumpeted new feature, for instance, is the new Retina Display that it boasts on its latest iPad. Claiming that it offers the best mobile display ever, the fourth-generation iPad also includes a different processor, for faster speeds. It still offers the functionality of earlier versions, of course, but the hardware tuning has helped Apple position the device very much at the premium end of the market.

Whether it's really enough to warrant a whole new iPad to be released will be debated for some time yet, we suspect, but the numbers don't lie: the new iPad has sold, and in great numbers, and it is, at heart, a terrific piece of technology. No wonder people were queuing up to get their hands on it on the day it was released. The suspicion will remain, though, that a new generation of iPad may be around the corner a little bit sooner than some Apple customers would like.

All that notwithstanding, there's little doubt that the new iPad has plenty of reasons to snap one up. Let's go through some of the technical details in just a little more detail…

Screen Display

There's no beating about the bush here. The screen on the fourth-generation iPad is just outstanding. The Retina Display is bright, crisp and high definition, and it's brilliant for watching movies on the move on. The screen measures in at 9.7 inches, with the display resolution far in excess of the iPad 2, at 2048 x 1536 pixels. That's more pixels than you get on a 1080p television screen that's five times the size.

Processing Power

For the first time in a while, Apple significantly upgraded the processor it used in its iPads with the fourth-generation model. This time, it's used the dual-core Apple Swift processor, running at 1.4GHz. Not only is this a more efficient CPU, it's also a faster one, and while it might not be twice as fast, as Apple may like to claim, it's notably quicker than previous generations in use.

Storage Space

Apple is keen to continue charging heavily for storage upgrades, which remains a real pity where the iPad is concerned. Its disproportionate pricing, when contrasted with the real-world cost of extra storage space, feels really quite unfair (there's a £160 difference between a 16GB and 64GB iPad at Apple's UK store). Of course, if you want an iPad with more storage space, Apple holds the monopoly on that. The fourth-generation iPad, therefore, shipped in 16GB, 32GB and 64GB flavours. Once again, it's on-board flash memory that handles the storage work of the device.

Battery Power

Apple claims that the hardware upgrades inside the fourth-generation iPad don't come at a cost of sacrificing battery life. As such, the standard boast applies here, which is that the iPad can go for ten hours between charges. Once more, this number comes down if you're using 3G or 4G for your web access. Furthermore, be wary if you're looking to play high-definition video. That terrific, upgraded screen may have big advantages, but it'll drain your battery in almost no time at all. Expect, with heavy use, around five or six hours out of your iPad before you need to recharge it.

Software Support

The fourth-generation iPad shipped, as the iPad mini did, with Apple's iOS 6 operating system on board, and all the software and apps that come as part and parcel of it. You can expect, therefore, to find the likes of Siri, the App Store, iTunes, Photo Booth and Video among the many default inclusions. Also, of course, you have direct access to the thousands upon thousands of apps that are included in the App Store itself.

Miscellaneous Facts

● The fourth-generation iPad weighs in at 652g. However, you opt for the 3G/4G version, that's slightly heavier, at 662g. It's slightly heavier than the third-generation model, and it's also 0.37 inches deep.

● Depending on who your 3G/4G services are with, the fourth-generation iPad has the option to act as a Wi-Fi hotspot. That means you'll be able to set up a wireless network that others can access, directly via your iPad.

● The device has two cameras built in. The one on the front is a 720p-capable, 1.2MP device, designed for FaceTime. For taking photos and shooting video, there's a more impressive 5MP camera on the rear of the unit.

iPad mini

Introducing 4G

It's the latest mobile data technology to hit the market and it's available on the iPhone 5 and some iPad models, but what do you need to know to use it? We take a look…

There's more than one way of connecting your iPad mini to the Internet. You can use a mobile phone service or you can hook up your handset to Wi-Fi. One thing you realise, though, is that Wi-Fi is the preferred option, because the 3G network connection that has served us reasonably well for the last few years isn't really all that fast. If you're trying to download an app, for example, you could be in for a bit of a data-zapping wait depending on how large it is. It has to be said that it is far from ideal.

Welcome, then, to the fourth generation of mobile broadband, which is finally here. For those who've used a 3G connection and noticed the trade-off of speed compared to Wi-Fi, it will be immediately obvious why 4G is such an important step forward. It is, quite simply, all about speed, because 4G is five times faster than 3G.

What Is It?

For those unaware, 4G is the very latest data network for mobile phones. It arrived in the UK on 30th October, 2012 when the company EE, the parent firm of Orange and T-Mobile, launched the country's first 4G network. It repurposed some of its existing bandwidth on a 4G-compatible frequency, which allowed it to initially launch in ten cities.

While that meant much of the country was cut off from trying the service, the fact that they were prominent cities (Glasgow, Edinburgh, Leeds, Manchester, Liverpool, Sheffield, Birmingham, Cardiff, Bristol and London) made a big difference. Since then, six more locations (Belfast, Derby, Hull, Newcastle, Nottingham and Southampton) have been waking up to faster speeds. In other countries, the roll-out is going at a different pace.

People using these services and seeing a little 4G rather than 3G symbol on their handsets are seeing the immediate benefits, giving users a rich media experience, with video and audio running at the same time all in the palm of their hand.

As an example of how much faster the new tech is, some tests have shown that speeds of just 4Mbps were found on a 3G handset and a whopping 45Mbps on 4G.

This has a major impact on what you do with your phone and it increases its usability massively.

First of all, you don't need to scour the country for a Wi-Fi network to get a faster download speed (although you will need to do this if you want to avoid eating away at your 4G data allowance). With a 4G-connected phone or tablet, you will have lightning-fast access to websites, be able to download apps to your device in the blink of an eye, work with Facebook without any delay and so much more.

There's no doubt that you will benefit from 4G given that all of us, at some point, will have bemoaned the slow connection that 3G has offered us to date. It really is time to change given that we're using the Internet on our mobile devices far more than ever. Watching a video on a 4G-connected phone is a pleasure that you just will not get on a 3G connection the majority of the time. It also cuts out a fair share of frustration when you and your friends are staring at a phone screen together praying the football scores will pop up before the next season starts.

Who Will Benefit?

- Commuters who want to work on their handsets and have access to a fast Internet.
- Gamers who will be able to enjoy more complex online multiplayer games.
- Film and TV fans, who will be able to watch full-length movies in high definition, streamed in seconds or downloaded in minutes.
- Football supporters wanting quick access to data as games unfold.
- Simply anyone who wants access to a faster Internet.

As more people switch to 4G, so software developers will begin to push out apps that take advantage of it. A new generation of mobile apps that can take advantage of faster connection speeds will arrive for the benefit of us all.

That's because with a 4G connection, you're getting close to the broadband experience that you have at home (unless you have super fast fibre optic broadband) but without the buffering messages, and with the ability to run more things at once and get through tasks with greater speed. Audio will be clearer and video calls will become far more common. Suddenly mobile connections are not the poor relation and the spin-off benefits to this become obvious.

Imagine, for example, being able to tether a 4G-connected phone of whatever flavour to your laptop to give you great speeds for work on the move, again without having to worry about Wi-Fi. Tethering is when you connect an iPad to the Internet via a mobile phone wirelessly. This produces your very own wireless hotspot at a speed that won't have you throwing your laptop out of the window.

Indeed for businesses and small companies, 4G is a real blessing. It allows for large and complex documents to be sent and received in rapid time and this can make remote-working a massive possibility for whole swathes of the working population. And once 4G reaches the entire country, it will make a massive difference to people who live in remote areas, because they will then be able to get a broadband speed that is far in excess of anything they have achieved before.

In the UK, EE plans to roll out the service to further towns, cities and rural areas in 2013, with population coverage of 70%, rising to 98% in 2014.

Getting Access

So how do you get connected? Well, first of all you'll need to have a contract with a phone service provider and, initially at least, that means being on a contract with Orange or T-Mobile and then upgrading to EE when the faster network becomes available in your area.

Before you take the plunge and before we carry on, however, consider these questions:

- Do you tend to connect to the Internet often on your iPad mini?
- Are you a large consumer of data (the faster you can access data, the more you are likely to use)?
- Would the Wi-Fi coverage in your area be sufficient?
- Are you in an area where 4G is not available?

Also, think about when you're commuting. Since 4G is not rolled out across the entire UK at present, the

FLAVOURS OF 4G

You may have seen another term used when describing 4G: LTE. This stands for 'Long Term Evolution' and it's the most consistent and speediest variety of 4G. The UN has set a technical standard for 4G and it's believed that LTE is the closest to that standard. It's also the one that is most popular in the United States.

It isn't the only system, though. There's also one called WiMax and another called HSPA+, but this is simply 3G rebranded as 4G and is not a true 4G. Companies using these are switching to LTE. For a list of LTE networks that are compatible with Apple's products, check out **www.apple.com/ipad/LTE**.

coverage will drop quite often, so a commute will not be quite the seamless experience you might want.

With all of those questions in mind, you may have decided that you want and need 4G, so let us look at the options for this and some of the pitfalls that you have to consider, starting with which Apple devices can actually handle 4G.

The simple answer to this is the iPhone 5 and some iPads, including the iPad mini. You cannot use 4G networks on anything else. The next step is to find a good deal, but that's not as easy as it may sound.

The cost of using 4G is inevitably higher than for 3G, but then progress is seldom free and much of this will be due to the vast sums of cash that mobile phone providers have to invest to provide the service in the first place.

The cheapest EE tariff for the iPhone (iPad 4G tariffs aren't available at the time of going to press) offers just

iPad mini

FREQUENCIES AND QUESTIONS

When Apple initially decided to adopt 4G for its latest generation of phone handsets, it chose to stick to just one type: the 1800MHz frequency.

The impact of this is that the frequency is only used by one company, EE, so it's only available to customers using the largest UK network, comprised of Orange and T-Mobile.

This was very much one in the eye for rivals O2 and Vodafone, both of which are pretty sizeable too, and that's because when O2 and Vodafone get their 4G networks up and running, they will be using a frequency that is incompatible with the iPhone 5.

Although Three will be using the 1800MHz frequency, O2 and Vodafone are bidding 800MHz and 2.6GHz frequencies, neither of which match, for instance, the iPhone 5's spec.

This came about because EE reassigned some of its old 2G frequency allocation to 4G and the 1800MHz band has been used by T-Mobile and Orange since GSM digital phones were originally introduced.

The reason why Three is able to offer 4G on the 1800MHz frequency is because it has bought a chunk of EE's capacity.

Whether or not this will continue indefinitely is not known, but we suspect that eventually O2 and Vodafone customers will be able to take advantage of 4G via Apple devices. Indeed, we would hazard a guess that Apple would make the iPhone 5S or whatever it will called compatible with both of these networks for 4G purposes. Later iPads, too.

The crucial thing is whether people walking into an O2 or Vodafone shop are made fully aware of the fact that any future 4G services by these two giants are likely to be compatible with the iPhone or iPad that they're buying.

500MB worth of downloads each month - the equivalent to two one-hour programmes on the BBC iPlayer. Customers who want to download more than their 500MB allowance will have to pay extra, with a user looking to download eight one-hour programmes a month facing additional charges of up to £180 a year. Ouch.

The EE deals range from £36 a month for 500MB of data downloads to £56 a month for 8GB of data. There are no plans for unlimited data downloads. Kate Murphy, at price comparison site **Moneysupermarket.com**, told *The Sunday Times*, "Customers who adopt 4G are likely to hit their monthly limits very quickly."

Currently 3G pricing for the iPad, at its cheapest, is £15 for 10GB per month via Three. O2 charges slightly more, for a 2GB monthly cap.

Providers

If you do want to use 4G, then you must be careful about which provider you choose. Again, in Britain, O2 and Vodafone have been late to grab their slice of the 4G market due to waiting for the outcome of the government's auctions, but when they do, you will be able to benefit.

It means people wanting 4G in the UK must go with EE or wait for Three's offer. O2 and Vodafone will provide a 4G service but, for reasons we explain in the boxout elsewhere on these pages, it won't be available for Apple users.

All of this is hardly the fanfare roll-out that you might have expected and the launch has been rather confusing in that regard, but the main point is that we have 4G even if the UK has been lagging behind other countries, which launched such services a long time ago (they include the US, Canada, Japan, Germany, Australia, Korea, Hong Kong and Singapore).

We've been using 3G since 2003, and the technology has become rather old now given the advances made with handsets and the demands we place on them. The good news is that your iPad mini is part of the 4G party and that you can begin to take advantage. By 2014, 3G will feel like very much the technology of the last decade and we might just wonder how we ever worked with it in much the same way that we laugh at dial-up Internet today.

SHOULD YOU WAIT FOR 5G?

We may have only just seen the launch of 4G, but moves are already being made to bring 5G to the table, and the UK is ahead of the game in this respect.

The University of Surrey has received £35m of investment from the UK Research Partnership Investment Fund, infrastructure providers and mobile operators with a view to researching the next jump in speed and bandwidth.

Academics have set up a 5G Innovation Centre with Professor Rahim Tafozolli saying the 5G will ensure mobile Internet will become indistinguishable from home broadband. Mobile communication is an important and growing area and 5G will take advantage of that.

Prof Tafozolli is the professor of mobile wireless communications and he already believes that 4G – which he said was worked on ten years ago – is now old. He believes 5G will be more economical and that the current systems are too expensive.

When can we expect 5G to roll-out? We wouldn't get too excited just yet, though, because the university doesn't believe we'll see it come to fruition until 2020. By that time we would expect it too to be old hat and 6G to be in consideration.

HOW FAST IS 4G?

	3G	4G
Data Throughput	Up to 3.1Mbps	3-5Mbps but potential estimated at a range of 100-300Mbps.
Peak Upload Rate	50Mbps	500Mbps
Peak Download Rate	100Mbps	1Gbps
Switching Technique	Packet switching	Packet switching, message switching
Network Architecture	Wide area cell based	Integration of wireless LAN and wide area
Services And Applications	CDMA 2000, UMTS, EDGE, etc.	Wimax2 and LTE-Advance
Forward Error Correction (FEC)	3G uses Turbo codes for error correction	Concatenated codes are used for error corrections in 4G
Frequency Band	1.8-2.5GHz	2-8GHz

DOWNLOAD SPEEDS

These speeds are hypothetical in that they depend on where you are, what kind of device you have and the signal strength, but it indicates the sort of time you will expect to wait when downloading files of different sizes.

	100KB	250KB	500KB	1MB	1MB
56k Modem	15 seconds	36 seconds	1 minute	2.5 minutes	1 day 18 hours
3G	<1 second	6 seconds	12 seconds	25 seconds	7 hours
4G	<1 second	1 second	3 seconds	5 seconds	1.5 hours

The Anatomy Of An iPad

The various iPad models are all slightly different, so here we've used the iPad mini to show how your iPad does what it does, just using the obvious physical components…

1. The Home Button

We should all be familiar with this by now. When you're sending a message, taking a photo, or using an app, you can instantly get back to your home screen with just one push of this button. Other uses for the home button include pressing it to bring up the search option while already on your home screen, tapping it twice to open the multitasking bar, and holding it down for a few seconds to access your trusty voice-operated assistant Siri. It truly is a wonderfully versatile little button, and learning all its uses can be a real time saver.

2. The Sleep/Wake Button

To turn off your iPad's screen, just press this button, which is tucked away on the edge of your iPad in the top-right hand corner. This is useful if you need to conserve battery power; you can either put your iPad to sleep or, if you won't be using it for a while, you can turn it off by holding down this button for a few seconds until the 'Slide To Power Off' option appears. You can also use the sleep/wake button to turn the screen back on when you want to use your iPad again, but if it's only in sleep mode, the home button will do the same job.

3. The +/- Buttons

Pressing one of the plus and minus buttons while on the home page will increase or decrease the volume of the ringer respectively. In fact, pressing these buttons will alter the volume of any audio that is currently being played through the speaker or your headphones. The plus button also doubles as a more conveniently placed shutter button to take pictures with your iPhone camera.

4. Orientation Lock

Above the volume buttons on the side of your iPad, you'll find a switch that locks the orientation of your iPad. Normally, turning your iPad on its side will change the screen orientation from portrait to landscape or vice versa, but if you flick this switch, it'll lock the screen to its current orientation – quick and very handy.

5. The Screen

The screen size and resolution will depend on which iPad you're using, but if it's the mini, you'll have a 7.9" LED-backlit display, with a 1024 x 768 resolution, with 163 pixels per inch. Every iPad also boasts a fingerprint-resistant screen coating to prevent smears, and strengthened glass

on both the front and rear panels. It's probably best not to test that strength out by dropping it, though, just in case.

6. The Front Camera

The front-facing camera is known as the FaceTime camera, because its primary purpose is to allow users to talk to each other via video while still being able to see the screen. The camera is centred above the screen, and can take 1.2-megapixel photographs or 720p HD video. However, it isn't the only camera the iPad has to offer...

7. The Rear Camera

There's also a camera on the back, known as the iSight camera. This can take five-megapixel photos, and 1080p HD video. It has a five-element lens and a hybrid IR filter, which might not mean very much if you're not into photography, but suffice it to say that it takes some pretty good quality snaps. There are a few more handy features built in too, including face detection, to focus on the important part of your photo, and video stabilisation, to smooth out any shakiness in your images.

8. The Microphone

If you're recording video or making a call via FaceTime, it might be useful to know where the microphone is on your iPad, to make sure you get the clearest sound. Well, you'll find it right on the top of your iPad, just above the front-facing camera, so if you are making a FaceTime call, you'll be looking and speaking in the same direction.

9. The Speakers

Unlike the iPhone, which has its speaker at the top so you can hear the person you're talking to when you hold the phone to your ear, the iPad's speakers are at the bottom. This is where you'll hear all the sound from your iPad, whether that's audio during a FaceTime chat or music, sound effects, or dialogue when you're watching a movie.

10. The Lightning Connector Port

When you need to plug your iPad in to charge or to transfer files, you'll need to plug your charger or cable into this tiny port, found at the very bottom of your iPad. The Lightning Connector was introduced with the most recent Apple products; it's smaller and simpler than the previous connector, which used 30 pins. The Lightning connector has only nine pins and is a completely different shape.

11. The SIM Port

If your iPad is the Wi-Fi-only model, this won't be there. If you have a 3G/4G + Wi-Fi model, though, turn your iPad over to see the slot where the SIM card is inserted. Like the newest iPhones, the iPad mini uses a nano-SIM card, while full-size iPads use micro-SIM cards. With either model, though, you'll find it's a bit fiddly to insert the SIM card in the first place; you'll need to use a pin or the SIM eject tool that came in the box to press the tiny button in the hole on the side, and then the SIM tray will pop out. It's not the easiest thing in the world, but on the bright side, you'll probably only ever have to do it once.

iPad mini

What's New In iOS 6?

Apple's iOS 6 brought in lots of new features, some good, some bad. Here's what you can expect from it...

Since launching in 2007 for the original iPhone and the iPod Touch, iOS has become one of the most used operating systems in the world. It's the only operating system that Apple will allow you to run on your snazzy new iPad, but luckily, it's also really good, and the intuitive, touch-based system has proved to be enormously influential both in the smartphone and tablet world. A new iteration of iOS, therefore, is always met with a great deal of interest, and the changes nearly always result in a some serious changes in the day-to-day use of your iPhone.

Now, though, iOS 6 brings over 200 improvements to Apple devices ranging from minor tweaks to complete overhauls. However, the majority of the iOS 6 update is focused on refining rather reinventing, with nothing included that is as game-changing as Siri, for example. That said, while many of the improvements aren't even immediately obvious, this may simply be because they fit in so seamlessly that it's like they've been there forever – features such as the new Do Not Disturb option, for example, or full-screen web browsing, or the very impressive refinements to the already astonishing assistant Siri.

Do I Update?

If you've only recently bought your iPad (or any portable Apple device, for that matter), updating to iOS 6 won't be an issue; it'll already be installed, meaning you won't have to lift a finger. If you have an older device, however, you will have to make a decision regarding whether you need to update to the new version.

If you have an original iPad, you'll find that your device isn't compatible with iOS 6, so you're stuck with iOS5. If you have an iPad 2 or later, the issue becomes a little cloudier. Some users have reported an unchanged or even slightly improved experience, while others says updating the new system drains battery life and reduces

performance. As there's no real consensus yet, it's up to you whether you make the switch, but generally, the older your handset, the more wary you should be about updating.

If you want to update, it couldn't be easier: just plug your iPad into the mains, then in Settings tap 'General', 'System Update', or plug it into a computer with your iTunes account loaded onto it and confirm the update when prompted.

Maps

The most controversial aspect of iOS 6 is its removal of the Google apps YouTube and, most notably, Google Maps. The transition to Apple's own Maps service has been a rocky one, with a number of serious bugs and data inaccuracies affecting the service in its early stages. Apple has apologised for the problems and has recommended users use other map apps while it attempts to fix its own service. Google, meanwhile, has been hard at work on a new Google Maps app, which is now available via the App Store, at last.

iTip – GET OFF THE GRID
Many of the iPad's apps use your location, but if you don't want anyone to know where you are, you can turn off Location settings in the Settings menu.

Built-in Facebook

iOS5 saw Twitter integrated into the fabric of the operating system; this time, it's somewhat inevitably the turn of Facebook. Facebook will sync your events and friends to your calendar and contacts, and now you can post directly to Facebook from the Notifications panel, Safari, the App Store, and any number of apps that choose to integrate it in the future.

3D Maps

One of the neatest features of Maps is its ability to render selected areas in 3D. Just pick your address (at the moment it's best to pick somewhere densely populated, as the service is still rolling out), then press the 3D button in the bottom-left corner of the display. Experiment by dragging and twisting the screen to achieve the best perspective.

New Clock

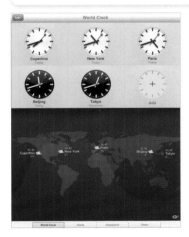

For whatever reason, the iPad didn't have a clock app when it first launched. Now it does! All the usual clock features are there: it tells you the time, it lets you set alarms and there's even a stopwatch if you need to time something. The world clock is probably the most interesting bit, and useful, too, if you're planning on FaceTiming with someone from another continent.

Share Photo Stream

iOS 6 now lets you share your iCloud photo streams with your friends. To do so, simply turn on 'Shared Photo Streams' under 'iCloud' in Settings. Then , load up the Photos app, select 'Photo Streams', then select the plus symbol. Now, you can type in the email address(es) of whoever you would like to view the selected photo stream.

What's New In iOS 6? (continued)

Find Your iPhone With Your iPad

If disaster strikes and you lose your iPad or iPhone, you can log into iCloud and access options designed to help you find it. The service will locate the handset using GPS (using its last known location if it's turned off) before giving you the option to send it a message, lock the phone, or simply make it play a sound – perfect if it's down the back of the sofa.

iStore Overhauls

All of Apple's flagship iPad stores (iTunes, iBooks and the App Store) have received big visual overhauls in iOS 6, with iTunes and iBooks getting a coverflow-style carousel at the top of the page that allows you to cycle through selected offerings before browsing individual categories. The App Store also has an improved interface, allowing better views of your search results.

Panoramic Camera Shots

The iPhone got the ability to take panoramic camera shots in iOS 6. Open Camera, select 'Options', then 'Panorama'. Then, take your camera and sweep it across the scene you want to capture, while attempting to keep the on-screen arrow in the centre as much as possible. Sadly, the iPad doesn't yet have this feature, but we're expecting it soon.

Do Not Disturb

By simply turning this feature on in Settings, you can block out the world and get on with that important work (*Angry Birds*, panda YouTube videos, etc.) without being disturbed by calls. You can even set it so that Do Not Disturb becomes active during certain time periods in the day. Set it to be active during the small hours for an effective 'sleep' mode.

iTip – LONG DOWNLOADS

Depending on your internet service provider, it's generally quicker to pause big downloads, and activate them at off-peak times

Reading List

If you find yourself web browsing but unable to read everything you'd like in one sitting or you're forced to move somewhere where there's no Internet signal, now you can save web pages and PDFs by adding them to your reading list. It's as easy as tapping the shortcut button and selecting 'Add to Reading List', then you can access it offline by tapping the open book icon in Safari.

Guided Access

Sometimes, friends or family will want to play with your iPad, but you don't want them having access to everything on it. To restrict access to apps or even to different parts of the screen, go to Settings, then 'General', 'Accessibility' and turn on 'Guided Access'. Select the app you want to use it with, then triple-tap the home button to call up options and restrictions.

iCloud Tabs In Safari

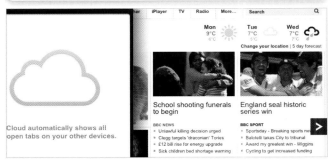

The web browser on your iPad syncs with iCloud, which means you can open the same tabs you were looking at on your iPad on any computer you like. So if you started reading a long article on your iPad and want to finish it on your PC, you can; if you start reading something at home, you can sync it and finish it on your iPad later.

Teach Siri Things

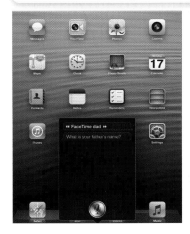

Siri is even more eerily intelligent this time around. If you feel comfortable opening yourself up to it, then you can even teach it about your relationships. For example, if you tell Siri "David is my dad", from then onwards when you say "Text my dad", Siri will identify the correct contact. You can also give him access to your Facebook and Twitter accounts.

iCloud – The Future Of Storage

It seems like a ridiculous concept: storing your photos, documents and other files in thin air? Yet cloud storage really is the future – a future that Apple is pioneering with iCloud…

In truth, it's the name that makes it all sound more fantastic than it actually is. Cloud storage? As in, those fluffy white things up in the air? How does that work then? And so the conversation goes on, with people getting more and more confused as to how the future of computer storage and accessibility is linked to what is essentially nothing but thin air.

Thankfully, the cloud element is just a misnomer and the reality of it all is much more conventional. Essentially, cloud storage is as much about accessibility and security for users as it is about being able to store files. It's a method of being able to access and use almost anything you create at any time, in any place, as well as having everything you do backed up automatically without you even lifting a finger. Think of it as a giant off-site hard drive, constantly plugged in and waiting to either store new files or provide you with access to older files you put there earlier. In fact, it's not all that different to using a portable hard drive on your computer at home… except the hard drive can be a thousand miles away from your computer and there's someone else doing all the uploading and downloading for you, that is.

Up, Up And Away

Although cloud saving's been around for a while now, it's Apple that's managed to bring it to the masses with iCloud. Built directly into the backbone of iOS 6, iCloud is a free service provided by Apple that directly links every iOS 5-running Apple device you own (iPhones, iPads and iPod Touches), as well as Mac computers running the OS X Lion operating system and any computer that you choose to log into iCloud with. All you have to do is create and activate an iCloud account on each device/Mac and choose which services can access that account, then go about your business taking photos, creating reminders, buying things from the App Store and much, much more. And while you're doing that, iCloud's constantly taking notes, saving files and generally making sure everything's kept in sync with everything else.

The real charm, of course, is that you can then access everything linked to your iCloud from any linked device. Want to see photos taken with your iPhone on your iPad? Easy. Need reminders set on your Mac to pop up on your iPhone? Done. Downloaded a song from iTunes on your iPad but fancy listening to it on your Mac? Piece of cake. And even better, you can access much of your iCloud content from any other computer as long as you have your email and password details, just by visiting the iCloud website. Hence, the cloud reference: your content can be plucked from thin air, no matter where you are. Like we said, it's the future of storage…

Above: The late Steve Jobs showed off iCloud in early 2011.

Above: You can access iCloud from any iOS device and any computer.

How To Use... iCloud

Just as iCloud makes storing and accessing your content as simple as anything, so setting it up and using it is equally as easy. All it takes is a few simple button presses and you're pretty much done!

Step 1: Getting Started

Although it provides an impressive service, a basic iCloud account is actually free. All you need to get started is an Apple ID, but getting one of those is also free. You can sign up for one directly through your iPad, or you can do it through a computer with iTunes installed (preferably the one you'll be linking your iPad to, as it makes things a bit easier).

Step 2: Creating An iCloud Account

With your Apple ID to hand, you can go into the iPad's Settings menu from the home page and scroll down slightly until you find the iCloud section. Touch this and then touch the Apple ID box to bring up the virtual keyboard. Type in the email you used to set up your ID, then enter your password into the box below and press the large 'Sign In' button..

iPad mini

Step 3: Merging Your Current Data

After a few seconds where your iPad confirms the login details you've submitted, you'll get an alert asking to merge your current data. If you haven't used iCloud before, then you won't have anything to merge. However, if you already have iCloud set up on a computer or other iOS device, then agreeing to this will copy across all of your previously saved data over to your iPad.

Step 4: Locating Your Position

Immediately after this, you'll get another alert asking if iCloud can use the location of your iPad. This is important, because the Find My iPad app – which can show your iPad on a map if it gets lost or stolen – won't work unless you accept this. You can tap the 'OK' button now or you can pick 'Don't Allow' and then just turn the location-based settings on later instead.

Step 5: Changing Your iCloud Settings

Back to those flick switches: these are the apps and services that can be linked to your iCloud account. Not surprisingly, you can link or unlink each one simply by flicking the corresponding switch to the on or off position. It's as simple as that Each one you link will share all data created within it through iCloud to any other linked devices you own.

Step 6: Backing Up Your iPad

At the bottom of the iCloud screen are the Storage & Backup options. Your basic iCloud account can create a backup of your iPad mini, which can then be used to restore it if something goes wrong. Turn on the 'iCloud Backup' option and it'll do it automatically whenever you plug your iPad mini into a power source while it's connected to a wireless network.

iTip – AUTOMATIC DOWNLOADS
If you link your app, music and video purchases to iCloud, then anything that you buy from the App or iTunes store automatically downloads to all of your linked devices.

Step 7: Buying More Storage

A free iCloud account comes with 5GB of storage space included. While that doesn't sound like much, it's actually a lot more than you'd think. If it's not quite enough to hold all your documents and data, though, you can always add an extra 10, 20 or 50GB for a yearly subscription. Tap 'Change Storage Plan' and then choose from the list that appears if you want to do so.

Step 8: Managing Your iCloud Storage

On the Storage & Backup screen, tapping 'Manage Storage' enables you to see how your iPad's storage is being used. Touching anything on the list reveals more details, along with an 'Edit' button. Use this to select and then delete anything you don't want to keep. You can also edit the settings of your iPad backup to change what gets backed up and what doesn't.

Step 9: Accessing iCloud On Your iPad

Not surprisingly, accessing any linked content from iCloud is as simple as using the app that it's linked to. Mail accesses emails; Contacts shares all your numbers and addresses; Calendar and Reminders transfer appointments, meetings, alarms and alerts; Photos keeps a backup of every picture added to your Photo Stream in the last 30 days and so on.

Step 10: Using A Computer With iCloud

Helpfully, you can access certain elements of your iCloud account from any computer, anywhere in the world. Go to **www.icloud.com** and enter your Apple ID email and password, then click one of the five icons - Mail, Contacts, Calendar, Find My iPad or iWork - to access any of the content that you've linked to iCloud.

iPad mini

25

Your iPad mini And...
Getting Started

If you ever get the chance to read the excellent biography of the late Apple boss Steve Jobs, you'll get an idea as to just how much effort the firm put into designing the packaging for its products. Exhaustive effort and a lot of research was put in to ensure that from the very moment you took your Apple purchase home, it felt like it was something a little bit special (as it should be, given the price tag you're expected to pay!)

As a result of all of this work, every Apple product is simple to get out of the box, simple to switch on, and simple to get up and running. It feels as if virtually everything has been thought of.

But here's the thing. Once it's actually out of the box, what do you need to do then? It's a good question, and it's one that Apple doesn't really provide much of an answer for.

That, then, is where we come in. Across this chapter, we'll be going through the initialisation basics that you need to know about. We'll be dealing with little jobs that need to be done to make sure that your iPad mini is set up just the way you want it to be.

As such, we're going to be covering getting connected to the Internet, for instance, as well as setting yourself up with an Apple ID (the benefits of which we're also going to be going into as well). We have tips for you to help prolong the battery life of your iPad mini, and we're going to help you get it nice and secure too.

We're also going to take a bit of time to go through getting your home computer and iPad mini working hand in hand, and what the advantages of doing so are. The two are designed to work together to a degree, after all.

By the time you get to the end of this chapter, then, the basic settings of your iPad mini should be firmly in place, and lots of the fiddly jobs will be done and dusted, leaving you free to get on with using your new purchase for the reasons you bought it in the first place!

How To Use... Set Up Your iPad

Yes, your new iPad mini is a lovely bit of kit, but there's one thing you might notice when you open the box: there's no manual. How do you set up your iPad for use?

Step 1: Language And Location

Plug your iPad into the wall using the USB cable and plug adapter provided, then turn it on. Start by choosing your language and location. These may default to specific settings depending on where you bought your iPad. Next, choose 'Enable Location Services' to make apps like Maps and Find My iPhone work properly.

Step 2: Setting Up Wi-Fi

Although certain iPads use the 3G/4G network to access the Internet, most of us will use a wireless network. If you're setting up your iPad mini in a place with Wi-Fi access, you can detect and configure this on the next screen. Using Wi-Fi is preferable, as it's faster and won't lead to you incurring hefty 3G/4G charges from your service provider if you have a data limit in place.

iTip – AIRPLANE MODE
If you're going on a plane but don't want to turn your iPad off, go into Settings and flick the Airplane Mode switch to On, making your iPad safe for use in flight.

Step 3: Restoring From A Back-Up

If the iPad you've bought has iOS 6 installed (which it will if it's a new iPad), then after a short activation period you'll get the option to restore from an iCloud or iTunes backup. This is obviously only appropriate if you've previously owned and backed up an iPad – if you haven't, you just need to choose 'Set Up As A New iPad' to continue.

Step 4: Signing In With An Apple ID

The next screen prompts you to create an Apple ID, which you'll need to use a large number of apps and services on your iPad. If you already have one from using an iPod Touch, iPad, Mac or previous iPad, you can sign in with it here. If you don't have one, though, choose 'Skip This Step', because we've covered how to create Apple ID for yourself over on page 32.

Step 5: Finishing Up

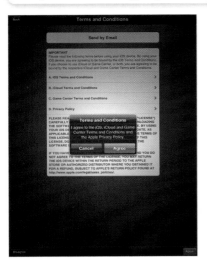

The next few steps are fairly basic, although you still have to do them. There's a terms and conditions page that you can wade though, but it's easier just to press the 'Agree' button (if you press 'Disagree', you can't use your iPad!). You can also choose to send or not send automatic diagnostic/usage data to Apple. We prefer not to, but it's up to you.

Step 6: The Home Page

That done, press the 'Start Using iPad' button and you'll be sent to the Home page, where all the iPad's apps and services can be found. To return here at any time, press the home button. You can use your finger to flick left and reveal a second page with more apps. The more apps you add to your iPad, the more screens you'll have.

iPad mini

How To... Set Up Your iPad (continued)

Step 7: Using The Search Page

If you flick the main home page to the right instead of the left, you'll find the search page. This is an all-compassing method of searching your entire iPad for something specific using keywords. Type a word into the search bar using the keyboard and anything that matches (from contacts and emails to music, apps, videos and more) will be shown in a list.

Step 8: Adjusting Settings To Save Battery

Since the iPad is demanding in terms of battery usage, it's worth adjusting some of the basic settings to make it last longer. Press the Settings icon, then choose Brightness. You can use the slider to dim the screen and save power, as well as turning on auto-brightness. Go back via the 'Settings' arrow, choose 'General', then 'Bluetooth' and turn it off.

Step 9: Using Pre-Loaded Apps

Your iPad already has plenty of apps on it that you can use. To start one, just tap the relevant icon on the home page. We've laid out extensive details of using many pre-loaded apps throughout this book. For instance, you'll find Safari on page 46, music from page 66, photography from page 118, FaceTime on page 154 email on page 156 and maps from page 172.

Step 10: Simple Finger Gestures

The iPad uses many different finger gestures as control methods. Swiping is easy: touch the screen, then move left, right, up or down to scroll pages, lists and other things that are bigger than the screen. Pinching is used to zoom in and out: using two fingers, touch and then pinch in or stretch out. This is used by apps like Photos and Maps, amongst others.

iTip – RENAMING YOUR iPAD
Go to 'Settings', 'General', 'About' and touch the 'Name' panel to rename your phone. This is what will show up when linking to a computer or using personal hotspots.

Step 11: Changing View Orientation

Although the home page of your iPad mini is locked by default to a portrait (vertical) view, many apps let you turn the iPad on its side and automatically use a landscape (horizontal) view instead. To prevent this perspective switch from happening by accident though, you can lock the portrait view in the Settings menu, under the 'General' heading. As simple as that!

Step 12: Setting Up Security

To set a password to prevent use of your iPad if it's lost or stolen, go to 'Settings', 'General', 'Passcode Lock' and tap 'Turn Passcode On', then select a four-digit passcode. Be sure to remember it! If you turn off 'Simple Passcode', you can set a more complex password. You can also set your iPad to automatically wipe itself after ten incorrect code entries.

Step 13: Restricting iPad Use

If you allow other people or children to use your iPad, it's wise to set up some restrictions on the use of various apps. Go to 'Settings', 'General', 'Restrictions' and tap 'Enable Restrictions', then flick the switches to either on or off depending on what you want to lock out. Putting restrictions on adding/ deleting apps is a good idea, as is restricting the use of Safari, for added peace of mind.

Step 14: Make It More Accessible

Also in the Settings menu, you'll find some accessibility options. Here, you can set it so that your iPad can read text aloud, or you can make the default text size much bigger. Both of these options might be helpful if your eyesight isn't very good. In the same menu, you'll also find audio and colour settings, so you can make your iPad work in a way that's best for you.

iPad mini

How To Use... An Apple ID

Apple ID is the one-stop passport to using all kinds of apps and services on your iPad. Without one, you're pretty much stuck. Thankfully, getting your account set up is a piece of cake - and it's free too!

Step 1: Why You Need An Apple ID

It's perfectly possible to get by without having an Apple ID, but you'll be missing out on a lot of content (and some apps won't even work properly!). Without one, you can't use the App Store, iTunes, iCloud and a lot of other apps, so it's worth setting one up immediately. Thankfully, it's totally free and it only takes a couple of minutes; you can even do it through your iPad mini.

Step 2: Creating A New Apple ID

There are several apps that allow you to create a new Apple ID (such as the App Store, for instance), but it's easiest to do it through iCloud. Go to 'Settings', 'iCloud' and tap 'Get A Free Apple ID' at the bottom. This brings up a screen asking for your date of birth. Enter it and then press 'Next' to reach a screen asking for your full name. Type that in and press the 'Next' button again.

iTip – DELETING APPLE ID ACCOUNTS
Although pressing the red 'Delete Account' button at the bottom of the iCloud settings will delete it from your phone, it *won't* delete the account from existence!

Step 3: Pick An Email Address

Next, you'll be asked to choose whether to use your current email address to sign up or create a new iCloud email address. If you want to use your existing email address, choose that option and press 'Next'. The next screen will prompt you to enter your email address, and then you can press 'Next' and carry on filling in the rest of your details (including setting a password).

Step 4: Getting A Free Email Account

If you don't have an email account already or you want to set up a fresh one specifically for your iPad, you can get a free @icloud.com account directly from Apple. Select the 'Get A Free @icloud.com Email Address' option and type what you'd like it to be into the box below. Try to make it unique, because if that address is already in use, you'll have to start the process all over again.

Step 5: Finishing Up

You'll be asked for a few more details, and then the terms and conditions will appear. Agree to these and you're done! If you chose to create an @icloud.com email address, that account is now added to your iPad's Email app; if you used an existing one, you'll need to check the inbox of that address for a confirmation email and click the link to verify it as yours before iCloud will be active.

Step 6: What To Use Your Apple ID For

With your Apple ID set up, you can use your iPad to do plenty of things. For instance, if you're going to use it to play games, it's worth going into the Game Center app and entering your Apple ID details to create a profile that'll store your gaming progress. And don't forget, you'll need an activated Apple ID to buy apps from the App Store too...

How To Use... A Computer With Your iPad

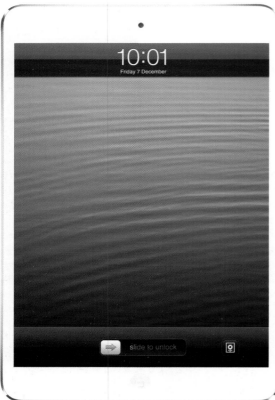

The iPad mini can download apps and iCloud can back up the content, but it's always best to have your iPad linked to a computer too for backup and media purposes. It's easy and free to do too... provided you have a computer!

Step 1: Downloading iTunes

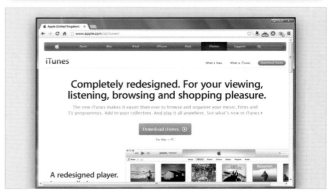

In order to have your computer recognise your iPad mini and let it transfer files to and from it, you'll have to install iTunes first. It's a free download and acts as the management software between your media and your iPad. Go to **www.apple.com/itunes** and click 'Free Download', then follow the instructions to get the right version.

Step 2: Plugging In For The First Time

Once you've installed iTunes, use the USB charging cable to connect your iPad to your computer and it should open automatically. You'll now get to rename your iPad and have the option to switch auto-syncing on or off. If you download apps through iTunes on your computer, this will automatically add them to your iPad too.

Step 3: General Connection Information

The summary screen shows all the basic information about your iPad mini, including a breakdown of what's on it and how much space it's taking up. From here, you can change the backup settings between iCloud and your computer, activate backup over Wi-Fi and also say whether iTunes opens automatically when you plug it in.

Step 4: Choosing Your Media Content

Each tab across the top represents things you can add to your iPad mini. 'Info' relates to things like your calendar reminders and contacts, 'Photos' are obviously photos taken by you and the rest are things that can be purchased from the Apple App Store. Music and video can also be added from your own private collection if you so wish.

Step 5: Syncing Your iPad

Whenever you plug your iPad in and start iTunes, it'll sync and any content on your iPad that isn't on your computer will automatically copy itself over for safe keeping. To send content to your iPad instead, choose what to send in the various tabs and then click 'Apply' button in the bottom-right corner to get the transfer going.

Step 6: Checking Your iPad Content

For more information about what's on your iPad, click to open the 'On This iPad' tab. Links to Music, Films, TV Programmes, Books, and Tones will appear on the left-hand side, and by clicking on each of these you can see what's on your iPad. To see which apps are on your iPad, you'll need to click the 'Apps' tab at the top. This shows a visual representation of your iPad's various home screens displaying its folders and apps.

iPad mini

Your iPad mini And...
Customisation

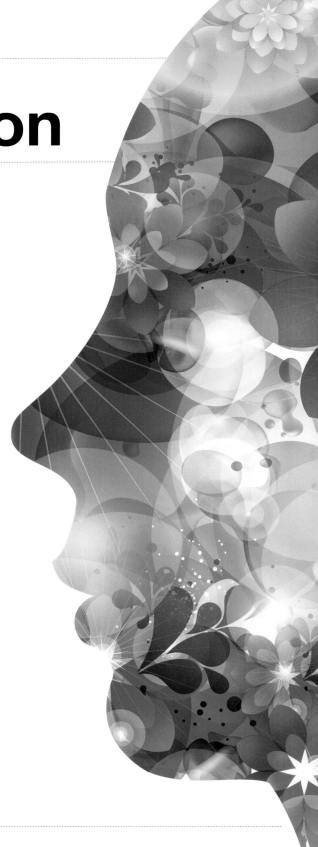

Right then: it's time to have a bit more fun! Once you have your iPad mini taken out of the box, charged it up, connected it to the Internet, and brought it up to date and with the correct settings in place, then you can start to seriously set about making it your own. After all, that's where the fun really starts!

There are so many ways that you can make your iPad mini that bit more individual, and we've not even touched on the wealth of accessories that can give the device a little added personal sparkle!

What we'll be concentrating on here is the plethora of settings available to you within the iPad mini device itself. These settings allow you to tailor the device in line with your own personal preferences, and basically get it just how you like it. The options that can help you do that are what we're going to be exploring within this chapter.

So then, let's start with this: how exactly can you customise your iPad mini? Well, for a start, you can change the background wallpaper on your Home screen to something a lot more personal: perhaps a family photo or a picture that means something more to you, for example. This works in the same way as wallpaper on your desktop computer. We'll therefore be taking you through how to get the picture you want onto your iPad mini - be it your own, or finding a suitable one elsewhere - and how to set it just how you like it.

Then we're going to get our hands dirty with apps, which is where the serious fun begins. Nothing puts your mark on your iPad mini more than your choice of what you do with it, and the abundance of apps you have to pick from is bewildering. We'd wager that there are things your iPad mini can do - through a few well chosen apps - that you'd never previously considered that it could! To help you keep on top of your downloads, though, we're going to show you how to add and delete the many apps available to you (over quarter of a million!), how to keep them organised, and how to juggle using lots of them at once!

We have a lot to get through here then, as you might expect, so we'll get down to business, starting right over the page!

iPad mini

How To Use... Wallpaper

If you really want to jazz up your iPad's display, then using custom wallpaper is crucial. It can set your iPad apart from everyone else's, show off some of your own character and even be a bit arty at the same time...

Step 1: Know Your Wallpaper Positions

It's an obvious point, but if you don't know, 'wallpaper' is a term used to refer to pictures in the background of electronic device displays - the decoration, if you like. There are two wallpaper slots on the iPad mini that you can fill, giving your tablet a bit more character: the background of the home page behind the app icons and also the lock screen.

Step 2: Applying Stock Wallpaper

The iPad actually comes pre-loaded with a fairly large (if rather boring) selection of stock wallpapers that you can apply to either the home or lock screen (or both), which you can find by going to the Settings menu, tapping the 'Wallpaper' option and then 'Wallpaper'. They're all the right size for the iPad display, so they can't be resized when you apply them.

Step 3: Applying Custom Wallpaper

It's also possible to apply any image you choose as wallpaper, provided that it's already been saved in your Camera Roll folder. This obviously applies to photographs that you take yourself, but also images that you save from the Internet as well. This custom option also lets you resize your images by zooming in or out, as well as moving it to help decide which part of the picture you want to focus on.

Step 4: Downloading Custom Images

To get images from the Internet, load up Safari and use the Google Search box in the top-right corner to search for 'iPad mini wallpaper' by typing it in. There are plenty of perfectly sized user-created options that look great for you to choose from. When you find one you want, open it in the browser window and hold your finger down on it, choosing 'Save Image' when the option appears

Step 5: Applying Images As Wallpaper

To apply an image, all you need to do is go to the 'Wallpaper' option in the Settings menu and choose where the image is coming from. When applying custom images, you can move and scale the image first – drag it around with your finger, pinching to zoom in or out. Press 'Set' and then choose which screen you would like the image to be the background wallpaper for: lock, home or both.

Step 6: Creating A Home Page Image

While you can put any image behind the Home page, don't forget that it'll be obscured by all the app icons so you might want to choose something that fits. Creating your own image is a good way of ensuring it works. The size you'll need depends on which version of the iPad you're using. For the iPad Mini, for example, a good wallpaper is 728 pixels wide by 1024 pixels high.

How To Use... Add Or Delete Apps

At the core of the iPad mini are apps. No matter what you're into, you can find an app to match. And once you've learnt how to add more apps to your iPad, it's likely to become something of an obsession...

Step 1: Introducing The App Store

Your gateway to putting all kinds of apps and services on your iPad is the App Store. Whether you use the store on a computer through iTunes or, more appropriately, through your iPad mini, it's literally the only place to buy and download apps. The library is format-relevant too, so if you're browsing through your iPad, you'll only see iPad apps for sale.

Step 2: Setting Up Your Account

As you've already created an Apple ID, you'll have instant access to the App Store. However, you have to provide payment details to pay for your apps with. Go to 'Settings', 'Store', touch your Apple ID at the top, select 'View Apple ID', then tap 'Payment Information'. Enter your card details and address exactly as they're shown on your card statements, then press 'Done'.

iTip – RE-DOWNLOADING APPS
Any app you delete can be re-downloaded from the App Store. Just tap 'Updates', then the 'Purchased' tab and the 'Not On This iPad' tab to see a full list.

Step 3: Browsing The App Store

If we're brutally honest, the App Store is a bit of a nightmare to navigate. Yes, it's split into various genre categories (and further subcategories in some cases) and yes, you can browse via paid apps, free apps and release date headings, but that doesn't mean the best apps are going to be immediately obvious. That doesn't mean you shouldn't have a look, though.

Step 4: Using The Store Search

If you know the name of an app that you want (for instance, one of the many that we've reviewed here), you can tap the search icon at the bottom and type it into the field provided. Tap 'Search' and when the list appears, touch an app to read more. As there are many similarly named apps, double-check you've found the one you actually want before you download it!

Step 5: Downloading An App

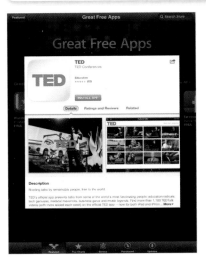

Once you're absolutely sure you've found an app you want, scroll to the top of the information screen and press the button indicating the price (either free or a value). Press it again when it switches to either 'Install App' or 'Buy App', then enter your Apple ID password as directed by the pop-up box. You'll return to the home page, where the app will download.

Step 6: Deleting Apps From Your iPad

To remove apps you no longer need, go to the home page and hold your finger down on any app icon until they all start jiggling. Now you can browse your home pages and touch the X on any icon to delete it, confirming your choice before it deletes. Note that you can't delete any apps that came pre-loaded on the iPad, only ones that you add from the store yourself.

iPad mini

How To Use... Folders

Having an iPad packed full of apps is fine, but the OCD in you might want to keep everything organised – we know it does us! Thankfully, you can use folders to sort your apps and even make room for more...

Step 1: Cleaning Up Using Folders

Your iPad can have up to 11 separate pages full of apps – that's up to 176 on display at any one time, which is a huge amount of content. However, since that can lead to confusion, it's better to group apps together using folders. This not only frees up space for other apps (a folder only takes up one slot) but can also make it easier to find the app you're looking for.

Step 2: Creating Folders

You can make a folder from the home page. Hold your finger down on any app icon until they all jiggle, then drag any app on top of another. Let go and it'll create a folder with both apps inside. You can then drag another app onto the same folder to place it inside. A single folder can hold up to 12 different apps at any one time, so just keep adding apps until it's full.

Step 3: Renaming Folders

Folders name themselves by default according to the category that the first app in it falls into. However, you can rename a folder to anything you want simply by tapping it, then tapping the white text field at the top of it while still in edit mode. Type your new name for the folder, then tap 'Done' to confirm. To exit the edit mode, all you have to do is tap on the home button.

Step 4: Emptying And Removing Folders

To view the contents of a folder on the home page, just tap it once and it'll open. If you want to remove apps from a folder, touch/hold on any of the app icons until they jiggle to enter edit mode, then drag the app out of the folder. If you move all but one of the apps out of a folder, the folder will be deleted and the space will instead be taken up by the last remaining app.

How To Use... Multitasking

One of the simplest and yet most vital things that the iPad mini can do is being able to run more than one app at a time. It can do it all: email to social networking, games to music and more besides...

Step 1: The Basics Of Multitasking

Multitasking on the iPad mini seems obvious, but it hasn't been around as long as you'd think. It was only introduced in iOS 4 and before that, only certain apps could be run simultaneously. Now, though, the iPad can run multiple apps at the same time. You can leave apps running in the background, and even have apps you're not using send you notifications to show things like new emails or Facebook replies.

Step 2: Using Multiple Apps At Once

Using multiple apps is a no-brainer: if you're using an app and want to use another, simply tap the home button and select the new app from the home page instead. The other app will still be running in the background. While you can theoretically have an infinite number of apps open at once, though, too many can cause your iPad to slow down, so it's not a good idea to leave everything running all the time.

Step 3: Switching Between Apps

When multiple apps are running, there are two different ways of switching between them. One is simply choosing the app that you want from the home page; if it's already running, it'll open up exactly where you left it. Alternatively, double-tap the home button to bring up the multitasking bar, and flick left or right to scan through the apps that are currently °running, then touch the one you want to open it.

Step 4: Closing Down Apps

The most important thing that most people miss is how to close down apps when you're done with them. Just hitting home may make you think they're shut, but they're still there in the background. To close an app properly, bring up the multitasking bar and hold your finger on an app icon until they jiggle. Now press the red minus symbol on the app you want to close.

Your iPad mini And...
The Internet

Arguably, much of the success that Apple has enjoyed over the past decade or two owes an awful lot to the Internet. Without the Internet, there would be no iTunes Store, no App Store, no downloadable music, and arguably no iPod.

If there was no iPod, then chances are the iPhone wouldn't have happened. And without that? Well, you get the idea. The basic gist here is that Apple has been designed its products with the Internet very much in mind for some time now, and the iPad mini is no exception to that well established rule.

While it's certainly possible to use your iPad mini without taking it online, if you deny it access to the Internet, then you're really missing out on a lot of what it can do (and, crucially, a lot of what it was *designed* to do). From downloading apps and keeping the iPad mini up to date, through to the sheer convenience of having email, web browsing and social networking on the move, it's a device that's been very much designed with the web in mind. Not least because you need the web really to get anything on it in the first place!

As we'll discuss in this chapter, then, the main way of getting world wide web access on the iPad mini is through Apple's Safari web browser. It's not a bad program either, and we're going to start this chapter by taking you through how it works, which may differ slightly from the browser you've been use to using on a laptop or desktop computer. Safari is more than capable, though.

That said, there's no need to worry if you'd prefer something else, because there are other web browsers available in the App Store. In fact, there are lots of other Internet-related apps in there, and we have a few recommendations for ones that are worth trying out.

As you'll discover, whether you're using the Internet on your iPad mini to keep on top of business or to make sure you're entertained, there are many, many options awaiting you!

How To Use... Safari

Apple's default web browser (the same one that's provided by Apple with its Mac computers) is simple to use and yet packed with features that make accessing the Internet a piece of cake!

Step 1: Opening A Web Page

With Safari open, tap the empty white box at the top of the screen to bring up the keyboard. You can then enter a web address and touch 'Go' to head straight to it. Note that the keyboard has shortcut buttons for '.com' and '/' to make entering web address quicker. If you hold your finger on the '.com' button for a second or so, you'll get access to more shortcuts like '.co.uk'.

Step 2: Opening Multiple Pages At Once

To open a new web page without closing the one you're looking at, tap the two stacked boxes in the bottom-right corner of the screen and then touch 'New Page' in the bottom-left. When you have multiple pages open, tapping the boxes icon lets you switch between them by swiping and then tapping one with your finger, or close them by tapping the 'X' buttons.

iTip – PRIVATE BROWSING
In Settings, turning on Private Browsing means that Safari won't keep track of the pages you're visiting. The frame will turn black to show you're in Private mode.

Step 3: Opening Web Links

If you want to open a link from any website that leads to another page within it or even another site entirely, just touch it and it'll load up straight away. However, if you want to open it in a new window, touch and hold your finger on the link. You'll get options including opening in a new page, copying the link to the pasteboard and adding it to your Reading List.

Step 4: Using The Reading List

You can also add pages to your Reading List by touching the arrow icon and choosing 'Add to Reading List'. To see the Reading List, press the book button and then choose Reading List by touching the glasses icon. You'll see all your saved pages, which are deleted as you read them. In iOS 6, these pages will be saved so that you can read them later even without an Internet connection.

Step 5: Adding Bookmarks

Unlike Reading List additions, bookmarks are permanent markers that can be placed on pages and then quickly accessed. View a page you want to remember, press the arrow button and choose 'Add Bookmark'. Tapping the book button at the bottom of the screen then opens the 'Bookmark' page; to open a bookmark page, just touch it.

Step 6: Important Safari Settings

Go into the Settings menu and scroll down to find 'Safari'. Touch it to access Safari's options. You can change the default search engine used in the top-right search box of every web page, clear your browsing history and clear any saved data such as cookies or passwords. It's best, though, to leave all options under 'Security' (near the bottom) set to on.

Related Internet Apps

Don't get complacent: just because you can read the Internet with the pre-loaded Safari app, that doesn't mean there aren't plenty of other Internet-enabled apps to make your browsing life easier…

Atomic Web Browser

Price: £0.69 / $0.99
Developed By: RichTech
In-App Purchases: No

If you're considering an alternative to Safari, Atomic is one of the best non-Apple browsers around. It's designed for touch-screen devices, making use of a series of gestures for control - though it also lets you choose which of 30 available buttons you want to add to it. If you want to try it without handing over your money, there's a free Lite version available too.

Free Wi-Fi Finder

Price: Free
Developed By: JiWire Inc
App Purchases: No

Using a 3G network is fine most of the time, but if you need to use larger amounts of data (or you have a tight limit on your mobile contract, as most people seem to have these days), then Wi-Fi's the way to go. By using this app, you can discover the location of free Wi-Fi spots almost anywhere in the world. Just follow the map, connect and then get downloading fast.

Dolphin Browser

Price: Free
Developed By: Dolphin Browser
App Purchases: No

It's not all about Safari, you know – you can download various other web browsers for the iPad too. As you might expect, this one does exactly what it says on the tin… well, apart from the dolphin bit, because that's probably illegal. Browse the web, simplify pages into text form, use gesture control, open pages using easy-to-navigate tabs and more – it's simple, but it does the job.

SpeedTest.net Mobile

Price: Free
Developed By: Ookla
App Purchases: No

Reckon your iPad's Internet connection is running a little slow? Find out exactly how fast it's going by using this free app. It's quick and easy to use: you just press a button and it tests your download, upload, and ping speeds in less than a minute. It can also let you know if your speeds are inconsistent, and it keeps track of your previous connection speeds so you can see if things are getting better (or worse!) over time.

Opera Mini Browser

Price: Free
Developed By: Opera Software
App Purchases: No

Yet another web browser for the iPad, this one's based on the fairly popular Opera browser for home computers and is designed for both high-speed surfing and data saving. There's even a built-in data usage meter designed specifically for people surfing the Internet on 3G models, since you can use it to see how much of your precious data limit you're using up while browsing. Handy if you watching video content on the move…

HP ePrint Service

Price: Free
Developed By: Hewlett Packard
App Purchases: No

Unlike the iPhone HP ePrint Service app, which allows you to print out documents to a wide variety of printing services around the world for collection later, the HP ePrint & Share app only lets you print documents to a web-enabled printer that you control. That doesn't mean it's not great – being able to print out those Keynote slides or Numbers spreadsheets remotely is a good thing – but it does make it slightly less useful.

Perfect Web Browser

Price: £2.49 / $3.99
Developed By: Vivek Javvaji
App Purchases: No

The iPad mini comes pre-loaded with Safari, so why on earth, given everything that it can do, would you want to put another web browser on there? Probably because choice is everything. After all, you wouldn't want to eat the same the meal for dinner every night or watch the same film over and over again, so it makes sense that you might not always want to use the same web browser all the time too. Well, possibly.

In truth, there are actually many different web browsers available for iPad (most of which are shown on the left-hand page!), but for us, Perfect Web Browser

is probably the best. It's not just that it seems to roll all of the things you'd want from a web browser into one package – bookmarks, the ability to view multiple pages, fast loading – but also because it does it in such an easy-to-use fashion and at a relatively low price.

Want to hide every element so all you can see is the web page? You can do that. Want to open hundreds of web pages at once without affecting the speed that the app runs at? Yep, that's there too. Need to sync your bookmarks with a desktop computer? Done. From extra-strong security settings and better memory

management to reduced data usage and a number of multi-touch commands, it has a huge amount of power behind a simple appearance and at a tiny(ish) price to boot.

Read It Later Free

Price: Free
Developed By: Idea Shower
App Purchases: No

Whereas Safari's Reading List still requires you to have an Internet connection to hand before it'll let you access the pages you stored for later, Read It Later can save your chosen web pages down into tiny text files and then let you view them whenever you like, even if you don't have a signal on your iPad. That's incredibly handy when you're going on journeys or going off the grid (which, for us, is pretty often). Just bring up the page you want to read later in a web browser, then save it to Read It Later – not surprisingly, the clue's in the title. There's also a Pro version available for £1.99/$2.99 that lets you view images and web videos at a later date as well, which is a bit of a bargain.

Scan

Price: Free
Developed By: QR Code City
App Purchases: No

Have you ever looked at a product in a shop or an advert in a magazine and seen a strange square pattern made up of black and white squares? Those are QR codes – special digital barcodes full of interesting data. Using Scan, you can use your iPad to read them and find out what they contain; from hotlinks to web pages or discount vouchers to recipes, videogame elements and much more, QR codes are a lot more than just funny patterns. Just activate Scan, point your iPad's camera at the code, line up the boxes and click! Instant connection to the data that the QR code hides, be it someone's contact details, a web address or something completely different.

PocketCloud

Price: Free
Developed By: Wyse Technology
App Purchases: Yes (Subscription)

Forget using the Internet to look for videos of cute kittens rolling around, hilarious jokes to tell your friends or naughty pictures of ladies. Did you know you can also use it to remotely interact with your home computer? Well, you can thanks to apps like PocketCloud Remote Desktop. Once you download the app, you can actively control your computer long-distance, open any of your files, access any of your software applications and more, so long as your computer has the PocketCloud client installed on it (and doing that is as simple as downloading it from the Wyse website and double-clicking the file). Seriously, it's so easy, even a child could do it…

iPad mini

Your iPad mini And...
Entertainment

If you want proof that there's an awful lot you can do with a comparably small screen, then the iPad mini is very much on hand as exhibit A. Its crystal-clear screen and intuitive touch-screen interface makes it a hotbed of entertainment possibilities, and unsurprisingly it's a device that many, many companies are targeting with their wares. After all, the quality of the screen is such that you can look at it for some time, without the dreaded eye strain kicking in.

As such, more and more people are turning to the likes of the iPad mini for their portable entertainment, and with very good reason. Apple, for starters, has thus targeted an abundance of material at the iPad mini through its own heavily-populated iTunes Store.

Through iTunes, you can get hold of music, download movies, get hold of full television series, rent the latest blockbusters and such like. Furthermore, there's also the continually growing number of further on-demand services, which allow you to watch live and catch-up television programmes, or listen to your favourite radio shows. Take BBC iPlayer, which now even lets you download certain shows directly to your iPad mini, so you don't even have to stream them.

In truth, the iPad mini is a terrific way to catch up on films and television shows, but there's still an awful lot more that it can do. Take, for instance, its Newsstand service, where you can get the latest issues of magazines, your daily newspaper or perhaps even the latest bestseller. They're all ready and waiting for you.

Over the course of this chapter, we're going to show you how to get the most out of all of these and, as always, we're going to finish off with a sizeable collection of app recommendations you might want to check out too!

How To Use... iTunes To Add Video

The simplest way to get TV and movies onto your iPad mini is to download them as you would music, which is why the built-in iTunes store offers more videos than you could ever possibly watch…

Step 1: Browsing The iTunes Video Store

Open iTunes and look at the row of icons along the bottom of the screen. You'll see a films icon, and a TV programmes one. Tap either of them to open the catalogue. You can browse for film/TV by category, or search by title, actor or director via the search icon at the bottom of the screen. When you find a film or TV show you're interested in, simply touch its name.

Step 2: Previewing A Video

Previews are available for more TV shows, while most films have trailers available that you can watch before paying money to rent or buy them. It's a good way to find out whether you'll like something, but be aware that the clip might take a while to load, depending on your Internet connection. It's worth noting, too, that prices vary between high-definition (HD) and standard-definition video.

iTip – VIDEO STORAGE
A 45-min TV episode in HD takes up about 1.4GB of space, and a 90-minute film uses about 3GB. Make sure there's space on your iPad mini before downloading.

Step 3: Purchasing TV Shows

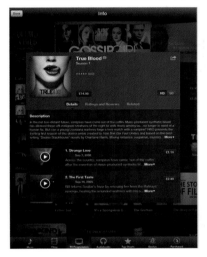

When buying TV shows, note that they're often cheaper bought as a series, rather than buying each episode individually. You can buy most episodes either in high or standard definition, but be careful: HD content will eat up a lot of storage space, so you might not be able to fit a whole series of a TV show on your iPad mini.

Step 4: Purchasing Or Renting Movies

Unlike TV shows, movies can be either rented or purchased, usually in both standard or high definition (which is better but bigger). You can also see a list of other films that viewers also brought in a similar style or genre by opening the 'Related' tab. If you're looking for something new to download or just want inspiration, these lists are well worth a browse.

Step 5: Ratings and Reviews

If you're still not sure about whether you want to buy something, you can find out what other people thought of it by opening the 'Ratings and Reviews' tab. You'll see an overall rating, based on all the ratings that have been submitted, and if you scroll down you can see more detailed reviews. Once you've watched something, you might like to leave your own rating and review too.

Step 6: Pausing/Viewing Your Downloads

HD content can take time to download and is best done over Wi-Fi; if you're moving out of Wi-Fi range, press the pause button to suspend the download until you get back. Once the download is complete you can go to the Video app to watch it. Then when you sync your device, a standard-definition copy will often be downloaded to your PC or Mac for backup purposes.

How To Use... TV-On-The-Go Apps

It's not just music and gaming that's gone portable thanks to Apple. The rise in on-the-go TV apps for the iPad means it's possible to catch your favourite shows in any place, at any time...

Starting out as a mere experiment, it's really quite amazing how the BBC's iPlayer (which began life as a website) has spawned an entire generation of 'TV on demand' services. Where iPlayer paved the way, now most major broadcasters provide TV on the move through software, and where once it was exclusively the domain of computers, now you can watch TV pretty much anywhere using your iPad.

While it's easy enough to catch the latest soaps and dramas, sports and some other live events tend to get left out of catch-up TV scheduling due to licensing issues (although there are ways around that if you find the right app). Mostly, though, you can find an almost full viewing schedule of either catch-up or live TV to enjoy and, even better, most of these apps are free to use. Indeed, only services like Netflix and LoveFilm require a monthly subscription.

> You can find an almost full viewing schedule of either catch-up or live TV to enjoy and, even better, most of these apps are free to use

Although some services allow you to watch content over a 3G connection – such as the iPlayer – most restrict you to a Wi-Fi connection to avoid excessive data charges from mobile providers. And while some apps from commercial broadcasters tend to come with additional adverts in them, it's no different to watching it on TV (bar the time and place of your choosing, that is).

More For Less
Meanwhile, the likes of Netflix and LoveFilm are challenging traditional TV services by offerings a wide selection of movies and older TV shows that you can watch whenever you want for a small monthly fee (currently around £5.99, with a one-month free trial period). These services work across all your devices including computers, games consoles and Internet-ready TVs, so you can watch a movie on one device and pick it up on the iPad app later on.

Above: The Channel 4 app has quite a good mix of old and new content.

Above: ITV's offering is fairly limited, but there are still some good shows.

Above: You used to have to be a Sky customer to use Sky Go, but not now.

Most streaming services often have special offers or vouchers you can enter on their websites or through app to get free content. For instance, LoveFilm is owned by Amazon and if you join via the Amazon site, it's currently offering a free Amazon gift certificate just for trying out the service, which you use to buy an iTunes voucher for even more content.

Since these apps all work on iPad, iPod Touch and iPhone, you can also share films and TV content with the family; if one person is hogging the big screen, there's something to keep everyone else happy too. Even better, if you have an Apple TV

iTip – STREAMING LIVE DATA

Since all TV-On-Demand apps stream data constantly from a source, it's wise to only use them over a Wi-Fi connection as 3G/4G connections are both slow and costly.

unit, then you can play content from the iPad with Netflix in HD and with 5.1 digital surround sound (when available) for that big-screen experience.

Of course, as these services become more established, even more recent and relevant content will be added to make them indispensable. With a huge number of categories and cult films, they form one of the fastest growing media industries today. More HD content is already being added to these apps and with an iPad HDMI connector (or via AirPlay and an Apple TV box), you can stream 720p HD content to your television, turning your iPad into a HD video player.

Above: Netflix offers a huge selection of films and TV shows.

Above: Just because it's on catch-up TV, doesn't mean you should watch!

The Sky's The Limit

Another app that shows a service provider breaking away from its traditions is Sky Go. Originally available to existing Sky subscribers only, it can now be accessed by anyone; all you need is a Sky Go Monthly Ticket, which is available at various price levels depending on how much you want to watch. Just the basic Sky channels cost £15 a month, while you can add sports and movies for around £40 a month (not much less than the proper Sky package).

> Sky Go shows a service provider breaking away from traditions. Originally available to existing Sky subscribers only, it can now be accessed by anyone who wants it…

The latest version of the app adds Sky Atlantic to the list of channels, while it offers the ability to watch over a 3G network as well as Wi-Fi. What's more, users can have up to two different devices per account, so you can run the app on your iPad, or use the desktop version to watch your Sky shows on as well as an on an iPhone. And, of course, Sky subscribers get all this included with their existing package; they just have to log into the app with their Sky ID.

With all this content available from the various apps, there's no denying that the iPad is rapidly becoming a pivotal part of how we watch and enjoy television these days. And since we can only get more content as providers realise the potential of the iPad, you can expect even more apps and content in the very near future…

iPad mini

How To Use... BBC iPlayer

Although there are many on-demand TV apps available, the BBC's iPlayer is the granddaddy of them all, and learning to use it means you'll be able to use most of the others with relative ease...

Step 1: Navigating The iPlayer

The iPlayer is divided into three main tabs. The 'Featured' tab shows off the BBC's top content of the moment with a list of the latest episodes; 'Most Popular' shows many of the same programmes but in order of viewer popularity; while 'Channels' arranges the shows by channel number and date to help find something you want to see from a specific time or plan your viewing.

Step 2: Finding Live TV On iPlayer

You can also use the 'Channels' tab to watch live streaming television. The current programme being broadcast will appear first and (if it's being streamed on iPlayer) will have a 'Live' tag. Tap that and you can watch what everyone else is watching on their big screen but on your iPad. Alternatively, drag the date bar to look at older content you might want to watch.

Step 3: Watching Live Television

When you're watching a live broadcast, the 'Live' tag will appear at the bottom. Unlike TiVo or Sky+, you can't pause live shows on your iPad; hitting pause means you'll rejoin at the current live point. You can find other shows currently airing live by tapping 'Live Channels' in the lower-right corner. Use the arrow in the upper right to maximise the video and tap 'Done' to finish watching.

Step 4: Information On Catch-Up TV

When you choose a show that's already been broadcast from the 'Channels' list, you'll see some detailed information about the programme, including how many days are remaining before it's removed from the iPlayer schedules and a list of similar shows that you might like to view listed below. Tap play to start watching the show you've chosen.

iTip – WATCH WHILE YOU CAN

Don't forget that shows have a limited life on the iPlayer, so you might not be able to watch something really old unless it's been repeated on the BBC recently.

Step 5: Watching Catch-Up TV

Unlike live broadcast iPlayer shows, you can stop catch-up content at any point and then come back to it later by tapping the pause button on the lower bar. Many shows also have subtitles if you have a hearing impairment or just need some help catching some of the noisier segments of a show. You can activate and deactivate these by tapping the 'S' button at the top of the screen.

Step 6: Listening To Radio

The Radio tab of the iPlayer follows a similar pattern and format to the TV side, only with stations instead of channels. Navigate to any BBC national station – or a date/show in the catch-up period – that you want to view and you can listen to a recorded programme. And naturally, the iPlayer also lets you tune into radio shows that are currently live on air.

Step 7: Adding Shows To Favourites

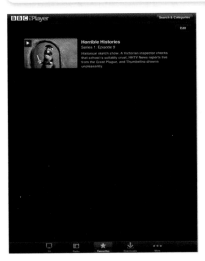

If you don't want to miss a future episode of a show, you can add it to your favourites by tapping the star in a programme window or by swiping a programme in Channel view and tapping the star that appears. All further episodes will then appear in the 'Favourites' page, making it easier for you to manage the programmes you want to watch in future.

Step 8: Setting Parental Controls

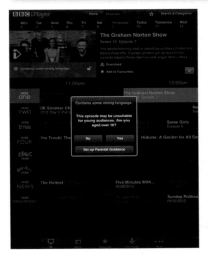

The first time you try to watch a programme with a Parental Guidance label, you'll be asked if you want to set up 'Parental Guidance Lock' settings. If you want to, you'll be asked to set up a PIN and create a secret question so that all content that isn't suitable for under-16s will be locked safely away. If you have young children who might use your iPad, it's worth setting this up straight away, just to be on the safe side.

iPad mini

Airplay
Who Needs Wires?

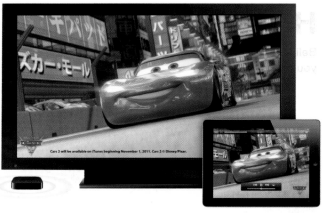

Above: Apple TV isn't as common as Apple might have wished, but rumour has it that soon there'll be Apple-compatible TVs with it built right in.

Just as iCloud is revolutionising digital storage, so Airplay is changing the way we play music and video in our homes. The only catch is that you need the right equipment before it'll actually work…

One of the iPad mini's hidden little tricks is something called Airplay. It's hidden because unless your house (or wherever you are) is equipped to use it, you won't get the option. If you do have the right gear, though, then you'll be ready for a whole new world of music, photo and entertainment sharing from iPad to all manner of other devices.

One of the main advantages of using Airplay through your iPad is that you can play music or video without the need to hook your phone up to a dock, allowing you to use it for other stuff while it's streaming your media around your home. When playing audio, not only does it transmit the music, but also titles, timings, album art and more so that devices with digital displays can show you what's playing and how long is left. Given that most laptop speakers are rather weedy devices, playing music through proper speakers improves the experience no end and while they tend to be sold at a premium, AirPlay systems instantly allow you to play your huge collection of digital music and video through them.

To enjoy your iPad music collection via AirPlay, you'll need to go shopping for a compatible audio product with the 'Supports AirPlay' logo. Several high-quality audio equipment

Above: Airplay can manage multiple devices at the same time, meaning you could have music or video playing in various places around your home.

> One of the main advantages of using Airplay through your iPad is that you can play music or video without the need to hook your phone up to a dock.

manufacturers like Denon and JBL have worked with Apple on the AirPlay project, so the equipment's always good quality (and a bit pricey too)

Don't Cross The Stream!

Once you've picked one up, you can set it up and start streaming your music around the house from your iPad using the AirPlay setting in iTunes. The iPad broadcasts the music and the speakers pick up the signal, then play it. AirPlay works over a Wi-Fi connection (not 3G) and you can stream to up to six devices, depending on your wireless capabilities.

As for AirPlay video mirroring (putting the same image that's on your iPad on your TV), you'll need to have a second-generation Apple TV, an iPad Mini and a wireless network. The Apple TV and your iPad need to be connected to the same wireless network and AirPlay needs to be enabled on the Apple TV for your iPad to get the AirPlay icon.

Using the Apple Remote app, which is free to download from the App Store, you can also use your iPad to control music or movies streamed through AirPlay from your computer. To enable the Remote app, you need to set up Remote Sharing on your computer's iTunes. Go to the 'Advanced' menu and click 'Turn On Home Sharing'. Enter your account details in the next screen, then do the same on the iPad's Remote app. It's a mite fiddly, to be sure, but the results are more than worth it…

How To Use... AirPlay

Believe it or not, buying the equipment is the hardest part of using AirPlay – once you've got all the gadgets hooked up, you can stream audio and video to them with the press of a button.

Step 1: Choosing An Output Source

Having set up your AirPlay devices or Apple TV according to the enclosed instructions, launch the Video or Music app to test it with. If everything's working, you'll see the AirPlay icon. Tap this button on your video player and you can choose from the active AirPlay devices connected to your network. Pick one and the video will be sent over the network to play on that device.

Step 2: Controlling Media With Airplay

With the iPad mini, you can also mirror your media content so you can see it on both your iPad and a bigger screen connected to Apple TV at the same time. Even on older devices, you can still control what's being played with the app's functions, effectively using your iPad as a remote control for your Apple TV-connected television or your AirPlay equipped stereo.

Step 3: Using AirPlay With Music Apps

Interestingly, it's not just Apple's own apps that offer AirPlay functionality; many iPad mini audio applications now support AirPlay as well, including independently developed music and radio players, music creation apps and many others besides. To transmit to an AirPlay audio receiver, it's the same as video; just tap the AirPlay icon and choose a destination.

Step 4: Multiple Devices On A Network

If you're lucky enough (or rich enough!) to have a number of different AirPlay devices connected up around the home at the same time, you can play music to all of them at once if your Wi-Fi supports it; just tick the particular devices you want to play music through. You can also stream audio to an Apple TV-connected television if you want to hear music through your TV set.

iPad mini

How To Use... Newsstand

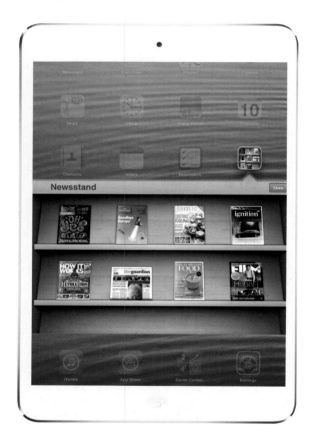

Why go to the newsagents for your printed publication fix when you have Newsstand? Use it to manage all your magazine and newspaper subscriptions, and even to download new issues all by itself…

Step 1: Finding Newsstand On The iPad

It's not actually that obvious, since it looks more like the iBooks bookshelf rather than a newsstand, but you'll find it on the Home screen of your iPad. The shelf starts off empty but expands to include magazines and newspapers as you add them. Newsstand is pre-loaded with iOS, but be aware that it can't be deleted or hidden in a folder if you don't use it.

Step 2: How To Download Compatible Apps

Note that Newsstand isn't an app; it just helps you to browse for published apps and store them in one place. To do this, tap the 'Store' button at the top corner. When you find something you want, tap the grey box that says 'Free', then tap it again when it turns green and enter your Apple ID. Just don't browse using the bottom bar, because it takes you to the main App Store!

iTip – HIDING NEWSSTAND
Not using Newsstand and don't want it taking up room?
You can't hide it in a folder, but there is a workaround.
Google 'Hide Newsstand' for video guides!

Step 3: Subscribing To Publications

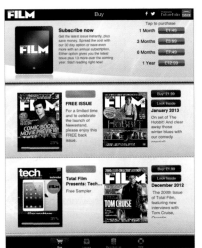

Unfortunately, each app's subscription method is different depending on the publisher concerned. Some offer pages to try out for free, but you'll always be presented with subscription options should you choose to read any regularly. Merely downloading the app doesn't subscribe you: that requires your Apple ID, so you can't do it by accident, fortunately!

Step 4: Reading With Newsstand

You can navigate issues of a publication by swiping the screen from page to page. Details will differ of course per app, but you may be able to zoom in on text or use a dedicated read mode that shows plain copy when activated. There'll also be a contents area to allow you to navigate through the magazine. Look out for icons that activate rich media or interactive features.

Step 5: Automatic Downloads

New issues of titles you're subscribed to can be set to download automatically. From the main Settings menu, tap 'Store' and you'll see where to switch auto downloads on or off (these will be there even if you haven't subscribed). Remember, stopping it from downloading won't cancel the subscription; you need to do that within the app itself.

Step 6: Deleting Apps From Newsstand

To delete apps that you've downloaded from within Newsstand, tap and hold one of the apps until they all start to jiggle, then simply tap the X button that appears at the top left of the app. Of course, you also have to set the subscription to stop renewing within the app itself before you do this, because just deleting the app from your iPad won't end the subscription.

iPad mini

61

Related Entertainment Apps

Entertainment is such a broad term, so it's no surprise that there are plenty of different entertainment apps on the iPad to satisfy your cravings. No matter what kind of TV or movies you're after, there's something for you…

4oD Catch Up

Price: Free
Developed By: Channel 4
In-app Purchases: No

As probably the UK's edgiest mainstream station (at least on terrestrial TV), Channel 4's app has some of the sharpest comedy from both Channel 4 and E4. It also has a catch-up feature (so you can watch all of a previously broadcast series in one sitting), guides to help you find the right show and parental controls if you want to let your children view something using the app.

ITV Player

Price: Free
Developed By: ITV
In-app Purchases: No

ITV's app has some content across the four ITV stations (ITV, ITV 2, ITV 3 and ITV 4) plus CITV for children. Despite that, though, the whole thing seems a little content-light compared to other stations, focusing as it does on soaps and reality shows (if you like them, great). However, there are also some classic dramas like *Sherlock Holmes*, *Inspector Morse* and others too.

Demand 5

Price: Free
Developed By: Channel 5
In-app Purchases: No

Channel 5's app has a host of Big Brother content accessible along with the last 30 days of other C5 shows to enjoy (if you can enjoy anything that Channel 5 puts on the air, that is). With impressive and uncluttered presentation, it's a good-looking app with plenty of quirky content from the channel's many reality shows, Aussie soaps and documentaries to enjoy.

Sky Go

Price: Free (Subscription required)
Developed By: Sky
In-app Purchases: Yes (movies on demand)

Sky Go is an on-demand TV app that's mainly designed for Sky subscribers, but you can sign up for a monthly ticket on the Sky site to access Sky without a satellite dish. The app provides viewing for up to two devices per account with the latest Sky movies, sports and TV shows on your iPad depending on the type of ticket you buy. It's also recently added Sky Atlantic to the app, which has some great US TV shows.

IMDb Movies & TV

Price: Free
Developed By: IMDB
In-app Purchases: No

The Internet Movie Database is an essential app for any film or TV fan, providing access to the latest trailers and movie news along with all kinds of facts and figures about the stars, movies and television programmes from both past and present. It also helps you find reviews and information about films you'd like to watch and what's happening on TV and with celebrities, along with huge amounts of film trivia.

Sky+

Price: Free
Developed By: Sky
In-app Purchases: No

Devotees of Sky's TiVo-style service will love this handy little app, since it allows them to set their box to record any program they like from wherever they are. With a seven-day TV guide available for viewing at any time, you can record single programmes or entire series at the mere press of a virtual button - well, as long as you remember to activate the record alert at least 30 minutes before the show starts, anyway.

Zeebox

Price: Free
Developed By: Zeebox
In-app Purchases: No

Zeebox brings social media and your TV viewing habits together in one app, in a way that it insists will revolutionise the way we watch TV. By that, we assume it means we'll spend all our time talking about the shows we're watching as we watch them, rather than just sitting down and enjoying them, and then talking about them afterwards. Anyway, you set it up by choosing your TV region and services (Virgin Media, Sky, BTVision and so on), and the app provides a guide to all the shows on.

Tap whichever one you're watching on the big screen and you can follow the streams from Twitter relating to that show on your iPad (which many TV channels have started promoting heavily both before and during shows), then talk with others and find out more about it, making it a powerful social tool for TV addicts.

Other tabs you can press include links to news and gossip about the show that you're watching or its case, while the 'Downloads'

tab shows apps, music, video or other related content that you can buy on iTunes, should you wish. Each show has a popularity meter and as new hashtags about the show appear on Twitter, you can follow them, thereby monitoring the discussion about a particular character or event.

Tap the 'Activity' tag to post your own comments to Twitter, Like a TV show on Twitter, Facebook or by email and, if you have an Internet TV, you can even control your TV using the app. You can also recommend the app to others and form a gathering based around your favourite shows.

StumbleUpon!

Price: Free
Developed By: StumbleUpon
In-app Purchases: No

Anyone with an interest in browsing the Internet to find the latest video of a skateboarding dog or baby falling over will have heard of StumbleUpon. It's basically the random dice of websites, uncovering all manner of bizarre content at the touch of a button. Not surprisingly, the StumbleUpon app works in pretty much the same way: you tell it what you're interested in and then press the StumbleUpon button to be magically transported to topical, interesting or downright weird sites, photos and videos that relate to your needs. As far as quick-hit entertainment goes, it's pretty successful, and considering the app's free, there's no excuse for not giving it a try.

Netflix

Price: Free (subscription required)
Developed By: Netflix
In-app Purchases: No

Netflix provides a huge array of TV series and movies to watch, all for one monthly subscription fee of £5.99. On the iPad app, you can keep on watching films you were previously enjoying on TV or your laptop or search for new films to enjoy from the impressive roster. Sadly, Netflix lacks the latest hits from the big studios, but it packs in enough content to make it worth subscribing to for a good few months (especially if you make use of workarounds like Unblock Us to access the US library of content instead of the rather empty UK one). With the standard range of categories to browse, though, you can also search for actors or key words in film titles, then just tap and play.

BlinkBox for iPad

Price: Free
Developed By: BlinkBox Entertainment
In-app Purchases: Yes (pay per view)

If you don't like the idea of signing up for a monthly subscription, then BlinkBox might be a good option for you. It's a movie streaming service that lets you rent or buy movies one at a time. Annoyingly, you can't actually buy things through this app; you'll need to do that on a PC, but once you've paid for your films, you'll be able to watch them on your iPad via the free app. There's a massive selection of films available, and new releases tend to arrive promptly, so if there's something you fancy watching and you don't feel like venturing out to the shops to pick it up, it's worth seeing if it's on here. There's one more catch, unfortunately: it only works over Wi-Fi and not 3G/4G.

Justin.tv HD

Price: £6.99 / $9.99
Developed By: Justin.tv Inc
In-app Purchases: No

The Justin.tv app is spun off the thriving Internet community devoted to sourcing live streams of content that might otherwise be locked behind pay-per-view barriers. It brings thousands of Internet video channels to your iPad for endless amounts of entertainment, with live events, foreign TV content, gaming events and more. Essentially, it's a little like YouTube, only broadcast live by individuals, companies, events or groups.

Of course, popular shows can have several thousand simultaneous viewers, which means the video quality will be down to the host's connection and the number of people viewing. Even so, Justin.tv can produce decent video-quality results thanks to its peer-to-peer sharing technology.

The service is increasingly popular with videogamers to broadcast matches and indeed, computer users are one of the biggest groups on the service. If you're watching something notable, you can make comments and join in a chat about the show or click the arrow button to share a channel with others or add it to your favourites.

While the 'Featured' tab shows off the most popular content, the 'Categories' tab offers social, entertainment, gaming, sports and news channels that are fully searchable if you're looking for something specific. You can watch all of these without creating an account, but it's free to do so.

Orange Film To Go

Price: Free (Orange contract required)
Developed By: Orange UK
In-app Purchases: No

Orange Film To Go ties in with the mobile network's long-standing free cinema ticket offers by giving users a free movie rental from the iTunes store once a week, every Thursday. That's not to say you get to choose what film you get – that's set by Orange, so you have to like it or lump it – but at least you get a peek at next week's movie offering into the bargain. The app lists the film on offer, lets you check out the trailer, a synopsis and reviews, and then gives you a download code for the iTunes store so you can grab the film. Rentals last 30 days, so you don't have to watch it straight away, but you do have to complete the viewing within 48 hours once you start it up.

Movies by Flixster

Price: Free
Developed By: Flixster
In-app Purchases: No

The Flixster app is a must-have for cinema lovers. With it, you can instantly find out where your nearest cinema is, what movies are showing there and what time they're on. That feature alone would make it worth having, but there's much more to this app. It's connected to Rotten Tomatoes, which means you get quick access to the opinions of hundreds of accredited critic and it will also find and stream trailers for you, so you can get a better idea of whether a movie is to your taste or not. It also lets you rate and review movies you've seen, and has a 'Want To See' list feature where you can keep track of anything you fancy seeing, and find out when it's showing near you.

Crackle

Price: Free
Developed By: Crackle
In-app Purchases: No

Crackle is a free movie service that offers a range of 'classic' films and TV series, mostly older or genre films with a few more well-known titles thrown in. Much like the matching Xbox 360 app, the iOS app enables you to stream content to your Apple TV via AirPlay too, so you can watch on a big screen – thankfully, it offers pretty decent video quality, despite the age of some of its content. You can add a choice of movies to a queue and watch them when you like or just pick one to play, and the app can alert you when new movies are added to the service. If you can't find something to watch, Crackle is a decent destination with some quirky programming.

iTip – IMPORTED TELLY
If you're looking for something different, try FilmOn Free (Free), which features a host of imported TV channels to watch.

VLC Streamer

Price: Free
Developed By: Hobbyiest Software
In-In-app Purchases: No

VLC Player is a popular independent computer media player that you can download to your computer for free; this Streamer app uses the same tech to stream whatever compatible content happens to be on your desktop over Wi-Fi directly to your iPad. It takes a couple of seconds to set up and then you can access all your VLC content and choose what to play remotely.

RunPee

Price: £0.69 / $0.99
Developed By: polyGeek
In-app Purchases: No

Got a weak bladder? RunPee can pinpoint the best part of any new movie to run to the toilet, so you never need to miss an important plot development. Via user-submitted data, it'll tell you which scene to miss, how long you can afford to spend in the loo, and exactly what you missed while you were gone. It may not be relevant to everyone, but for many people - especially those with kids!

GetGlue

Price: Free
Developed By: AdaptiveBlue
In-app Purchases: No

One of the best things about being a fan of movies and TV is being able to talk about them to your friends. GetGlue is a social network designed specifically for people who love to gab about what we've been watching: you can check-in when you're watching something to make a record of it, earn stickers, and find other fans who are watching at the same time as you.

Best Of YouTube

Price: Free
Developed By: Chris Software
In-app Purchases: No

There's so much content available on YouTube these days, it can be hard to find the good stuff beyond the Top Ten lists (even if you're using other apps like StumbleUpon to give you the drop on quality videos). Best Of YouTube helps find all that with voted-for content in a range of categories. From funnies to sports and magic to autos and science, you can find the best videos and even upload your own content.

Sky Movies

Price: Free
Developed By: Sky UK
In-app Purchases: No

The Sky Movies app offers guides to the films on Sky Movies, obviously. With it, you can add new movies to a shortlist, create calendar reminders of when a particular film is on and set remote record for your Sky+ box if you're away. The latest version also includes a cimema finder for big-screen outings, and also links with the Sky Go app so that subscribers can watch the latest Sky films on their iPad.

Remote

Price: Free
Developed By: Apple
In-app Purchases: No

We always thought the idea of a remote control was that it was meant to be small and unnoticeable. Still, if you prefer the opposite and want to turn your iPad mini into a working remote for iTunes on your computer or an Apple TV device, then you can download Remote and do just that. It's simple to use and can switch easily between devices at the flick of a button. Still, maybe it's one that's better suited to the iPhone or iPod Touch.

iPad mini

Your iPad mini And…
Music

Obviously, the iPad wasn't the start of Apple's domination in the world of technology: it was the humble iPod that came first, changing the face of portable music forever with its massive storage, ease of use and beautifully ergonomic design. While the iPad mini obviously has a whole lot more crammed into its portable frame, though, that doesn't mean Apple has forgotten what helped pave the way for it to happen. That's why it's no surprise to learn that the Music app that comes pre-loaded on the iPad does everything the iPod can do without even breaking a sweat.

Using the Music app is naturally a piece of cake. You can browse your music collection by artist, album, genre and more, then simply touch an album or track to have it play. From there, you can skip through tracks and change the volume (the iPad mini plays by default through its built-in speakers, but you can also use AirPlay as explained on page 58), as well as jump directly to other tracks on the same album by tapping the 'List' button in the top-right corner. You can even turn your iPad on its side to get the Cover Flow view, letting you browse your albums with a simple flick of the finger.

Of course, being a portable music device is just half the story; the iPad mini also comes pre-loaded with a portable version of the iTunes store, meaning you can download new tracks and albums at the mere touch of the screen. It also offers technology that can scan your current music collection and make suggestions on things you'd like that are similar – handy if you're the kind of person who can't decide what to try next. And yes, all of this runs in the background of the iPad's other functions, so you can be downloading tunes and listening to music while surfing the Internet, playing games or sending messages via Facebook and Twitter.

How To Use... iTunes

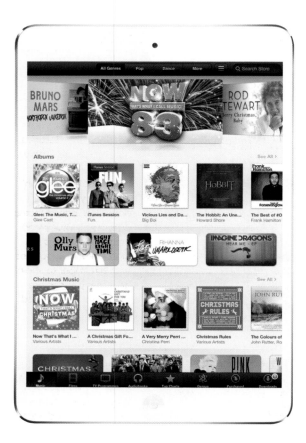

Although you can use iTunes on a computer to buy music, the iTunes app on the iPad makes it just as easy to get your music on the go and keep everything organised as you'd like it...

Step 1: Browsing The iTunes Store

Thanks to the iTunes app that comes pre-loaded on the iPad mini, you can easily browse through the wide selection of music on offer by Releases, Charts, or Genres with sub-sections for singles and albums. Alternatively, if you already know what you want, you can just search for an artist or song title by touching 'Search Store' at the top of the screen.

Step 2: Previewing Tracks Before Buying

To hear a preview of any track, click on the song number or name. It may take a short time to load up depending on your connection. Previews last 30 seconds and you can click the stop button to end it or on another track to preview that one, cancelling the first selection. If you're in a general view, you can double-tap a song to see the album that it's come from.

iTip – BUYING INDIVIDUAL TRACKS
If a track is an 'Album Only' download on one album, it may be available individually on another album. Search properly and you may find it in the store on its own.

Step 3: Individual Songs And Albums

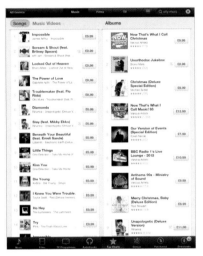

You'll notice that most songs have a price already marked next to them. Touch that price and you'll be able to download the song. Some songs, however, are only available as part of an album, and not individually. If a song is listed as 'Album Only', you'll have to click the 'Buy Album' button at the top of the page and buy the whole album to get the track you're after.

Step 4: Confirming Your Details

Usually, you'll be asked to enter your iTunes password to confirm a purchase. If a purchase fails, you'll need to go to Settings, then tap 'Store' Apple ID', 'View Apple ID', 'Payment Information' to check your card details are right. Once a purchase is confirmed, active downloads will highlight at the bottom with a number to show how many songs are still to be downloaded.

Step 5: Monitoring Your Downloads

If you have a number of songs downloading, you can follow their progress on the 'Purchased' menu. A number shows how many files are still to download and you can tap to see the file sizes and download progress of each one. You can't play songs through the iTunes app, though; you have to open Music to play your downloaded tracks once transfer is complete.

Step 6: Accessing Previous Purchases

If you've downloaded music to a computer or another iOS device linked to your Apple ID, you can click on the 'Purchased' option at the bottom of the page and choose 'Recent Purchases' to find those songs listed there. Tap 'Download All' to copy every file in the list to your iPad or just tap the button next to a particular song to download individual tracks instead.

iPad mini

How To Use... Your CDs On Your iPad

Buying new songs is one thing, but if you already have an extensive CD collection, then adding those songs to your iPad requires you to use a computer and the 'big' version of iTunes instead. Don't worry, though: it's free!

Step 1: Getting Started

First, put a music CD into your computer. If it's a Mac, it'll open iTunes automatically, while a PC will offer software to use, so choose 'Import Songs Using iTunes'. If you don't get such a choice, open iTunes manually from the Start menu or right-click on your CD drive icon in My Computer, then choose 'Open With...' and 'iTunes'.

Step 2: Choosing Tracks To Import

Once iTunes is open, it'll use the online Gracenote database to match your CD to the right track listing, saving you having to type it in yourself. Check it's correct – sometimes there are spelling or naming errors in the database – then deselect any tracks you don't want to import by clicking the boxes next to the track numbers.

Step 3: Changing The Import Format

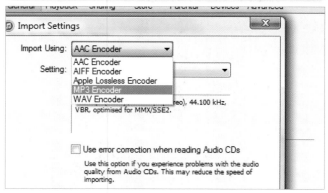

If you want to copy your CDs to devices other than your iPad, you can choose a different data encoder by clicking on the 'Import Settings' button. MP3s will play on pretty much any portable music device. iPads can play both AAC and MP3 files by default, so they're your safest bets when importing music.

Step 4: Changing The Audio Quality

You can also change the audio quality in the 'Import Settings' menu to import your chosen tracks at a higher audio quality (known as Kbps or kilobytes per second). The higher that is, the larger the imported files will be. Click the 'Help' button for a detailed explanation of the different file formats and what the various audio settings are for.

iTip – RESTRICTING EXPLICIT CONTENT
The Pad has settings that can prevent children downloading music or podcasts with explicit content. Go to Settings, then tap 'General', 'Restrictions', and 'iTunes'.

Step 5: Importing Your Music Tracks

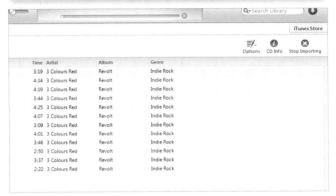

That done, click the 'Import CD' button in the bottom corner; you can monitor the progress of the import in the top window. Imported files appear with a green tick next to them, while in-progress files have an orange activity light next to them. A typical song takes around 30 seconds to import. To halt the operation, click 'Stop Importing'.

Step 6: Connecting Your iPad

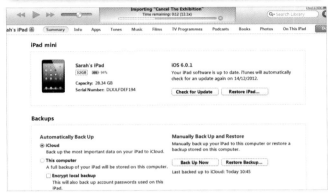

Now use your USB lead to connect your iPad to the computer. iTunes will recognise it and add an icon on the left. Wait for any synchronisation activity to finish first, then click the iPad icon to check you have enough space to copy over the new music files. If space is low, you'll need to delete some apps, videos, photos or music first.

Step 7: Copying Over Your Music

If you click the 'Music' tab at the top of the screen, you can tick 'Sync Music' and choose your entire music library, selected artists or albums to copy across. For more control, click 'Music' on the left and select individual or group of tracks, then choose 'New Playlist' From Selection in the 'File' menu; you can add this playlist to your iPad.

Step 8: Finishing And Playing

When your chosen music files have finished copying over to your iPad, be sure to click the eject button next to the iPad icon and wait for the icon to disappear before disconnecting the cable. Now you can open up the Music app on your iPad to see all the content that you've copied over. Just touch a track or album to start it playing.

Garageband

Price: £2.99 / $4.99
Developed By: Apple
In-App Purchases: No

The iPad Garageband app is scarily close to the full Mac OS X version, and it's a brilliant way to make your own music wherever you are, even if you can't really play any instruments...

Garageband for the iPad is like having an entire band in your hands. With plenty of different kinds of instruments and dozens of handy, easy to use tools on offer, it's a pretty serious music creation app. It packs a hell of a lot into a really small space. The fact that Apple is only charging £2.99 for it is pretty remarkable too, especially since the full experience (as part of the iLife package) is £40. Of course, the low price doesn't mean it's a small app; rocking in as a 500MB download, you'll need to allow a little time for it to install on your iPad. And once it's there, you might notice other differences too if you're used to the Mac or iPad version. However, that doesn't make the iPad version of Garageband any less useful. In fact, being able to take it anywhere you go makes it probably the most accessible version of the software yet.

> Although it's small and easy to use, don't ignore the power or features of the app for creating a serious piece of music.

At its simplest, Garageband lets you pick an instrument from drums, keyboard, guitar or bass, play around with them for a bit until you work out a tune or even a few notes and then lay something down. You can record anything you create on the eight-track sequencer provided and then add further instruments or samples to create a fully fledged tune. While it's small and easy to use, though, don't ignore the power or features of the app for creating a serious piece of music. For amateurs, various levels of autoplay allow the processor to help you create a pleasant-sounding tune by maintaining timing, while the number of synthesisers and effects pedals means you can make an original-sounding creation with enough tweaks.

Once you've experimented with the various basic instruments, you'll find that the guitars can play in chord or note mode across a range of scales including pentatonic, while the blues and electric guitars have a number of pedals that you can use to alter what's being played. Once you've found a decent sound, you can adjust the chords to something suitable and start playing.

Above: The amp tool does exactly what you'd expect it to.

Above: The drums provide a full kit for you to play. Smash away!

When you've mastered a tune, you can then record that snippet of music, move into the eight-track sequencer and use it as the basis for a full song, using short bursts of samples or audio recordings to go along with the instrumentals. While real musicians sadly can't plug in a keyboard, there is a feature to connect a real guitar through the iPad's headphone socket to record some decent string sounds.

For professionals and pro-sumers, GarageBand on iPad can also be used to import a range of existing samples, so musicians can create on the go. There are some samples stored in the app, but musicians will likely have their own they'll want to use, and the usual formats including Apple Loops, AIFF, WAV, CAF, AAC and MP3 files can all be used. Music can be exported in data or song form to be worked on using a larger device.

With a little effort and no real musical skill, it's possible to use Garageband to create a great sounding tune you can play on your iPad and share with friends. Beyond that, musicians can use their iPad in the absence of a real studio to create in the most unlikely of locations, whenever they get that buzz of inspiration.

How To Use... Garageband

It may be small, but the iPad version of Garageband still packs a punch in terms of being able to create great music tracks. Follow these simple steps and become a portable virtuoso!

Step 1: Picking An Instrument

Once you start Garageband, flick left and right to see the various instruments and effects you can choose from. Pick one of the basic sounds for your first try – either a Smart Keyboard, Smart Guitar, Smart Bass or the basic keyboard and drum kit. We'll start with the Smart Keyboard in this example, as it allows any user to create a decent track.

Step 2: Changing The Keyboard Settings

If you tap on the cog button in the top-right of the screen, you'll get to adjust the basic settings for each instrument, including volume, pan, echo and reverb. Quantisation and transposition help keep your creation on time and in key, while velocity changes how subtly the keys work in relation to your finger taps.

Step 3: Setting Autoplay

All of the smart instruments have an autoplay option, shown as a dial near the top of the screen. Set it to the lowest level and it'll play a simple set of chords based on the current settings; dial it up to higher levels and you get a more complicated tune that you can play along to. This will be recorded along with what you play.

Step 4: The Smart Keyboard

The Smart Keyboard, with autoplay turned on, breaks the keys down into simpler segments. Tap a key and that note will keep playing in time; you can even choose one from the upper row and one from the lower, making them both play at once. Move between them to create a pleasing tune until you find one that you want to record.

iPad mini

How To Use... Garageband (continued)

Step 5: Recording Your First Track

Tap the red record button at the top to start saving the first part of your tune. You can record short or long segments that can be adjusted in the sampler. For now, play until the timer moves to the right-hand side of the screen, then tap the stop button to complete the recording. Now tap the sequencer button, upper-left, to move to the sequencer.

Step 6: Using The Eight-Track Sequencer

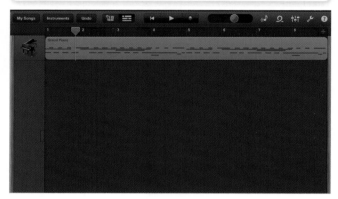

You can now see your recorded piano track on the sequencer. Press play and it'll play it back to you. If you don't like what you hear, delete it and repeat step five. If you're happy, it's time to add another instrument. Tap the plus button to add another track and it'll take you back to the main screen where you can choose another instrument.

Step 7: Playing The Smart Guitar

With the Smart Guitar, you tap a chord on the appropriate string to play the instrument; with the Basic Guitar, you can bend the strings for a more individual sound. Steps three to six above still apply, so repeat them to change settings and the autoplay level, then record a new track. Again, tap on the sequencer button to view what you create.

Step 8: Adding A Drum Track

Tap the plus button on the sequencer again, but this time choose 'Smart Drums' from the 'Instrument' menu. To add drums, just drag sounds to appropriate places on the grid. There's even a random option (the dice button) to help you start off. There's no autoplay option here, so just mess around with the effects and record to add to your song.

Step 9: Testing And Adding Samples

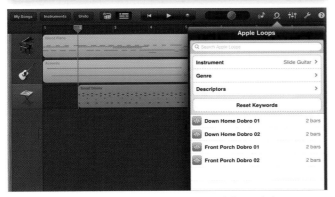

In the Sequencer, tap the loop icon (upper-left) and choose 'Apple Loops'. These are short, snappy recordings that can be added to your track. Browse until you find one you like, then touch to give it a try. To add one to the sequencer, touch and hold on the left-hand icon before dropping it into an empty track when one appears.

Step 10: Working In The Sequencer

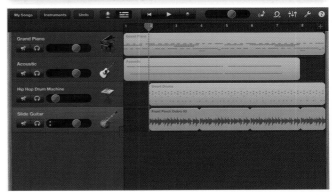

While you're using the sequencer to try to clean up your track, things can get rather noisy. Thankfully, you can tune out some tracks by dragging the instrument list to the right to reveal the audio options for each track. Here, you can mute, lower or raise the volume level of each individual track. To go back to the sequencer, flick left.

Step 11: Moving And Shortening Tracks

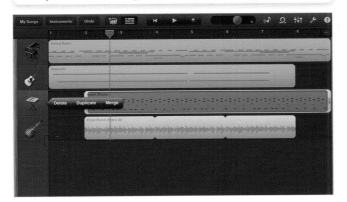

You can shorten a track sequence by touching and dragging the right-hand edge to the left. You can move a sequence by dragging it across the timeline, and if you decide you don't like one track, you can tap on the instrument and choose 'Delete'. You can also copy a track by choosing 'Duplicate' to make a variation instead.

Step 12: Outputting Your Track

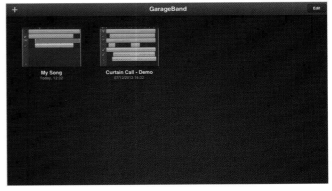

Songs are automatically saved when you quit Garageband, but you can click on the arrow icon (top left on the sequencer) at any time and choose 'My Songs' to see your creations. From here, you can choose to export your song to iTunes or share it by email, which will send a finalised audio version of the track to the address of your choosing.

Related Music Apps

With music being a good part of the services that the iPad mini offers, it's no surprise that there's a huge range of both music creation and playing apps available for it to cater for audiophiles everywhere…

My First Orchestra App

Price: £2.99
Developed By: Naxos Digital Services Ltd
In-app Purchases: No

Give your kids a taste for classical music with this surprisingly fun music app. Tormod the Troll gives users a tour of the orchestra, offering a cute introduction to what each instrument looks and sounds like. There's a full album's worth of classical music included, and by touching any of the text in the game, kids can hear it read aloud, so they don't even need to be able to read to find out what a cello is.

Spotify

Price: Free
Developed By: Spotify
In-app Purchases: Yes (music)

Want a massive music collection without having to download it onto your iPad? Then Spotify is the answer. This iPad version, which takes full advantage of the extra screen real estate, allows you to take over 15 million songs on the go with both streaming and offline modes. You need to be subscribe once the free trial is over, but it's well worth it for a world of tunes.

Beat_Machine

Price: Free
Developed By: Intermediaware
In-app Purchases: Yes (more tracks / drums)

Ignore the fact that this one's been filed under Games rather than Music on the App Store; Beat_Machine is definitely a full-on drum machine with all manner of different effects to choose from. Load it up and your iPad screen becomes a multi-purpose drum pad with various sounds. You can then load in new sound effects using in-app purchases and add loops for extra creativity.

Filtatron

Price: £5.49 / $7.99
Developed By: Moog
In-app Purchases: No

In case you didn't already know, Moog is something of a big name in synthesisers and its iPad app brings all its knowledge under the power of your finger with a sampler, plus a range of amp, delay, filter, feedback, frequency and other settings that you can adjust with a finger tap. Definitely an app for the mad musical experimenter in you, although there's no denying that the price is a little high. But what price can you put on creativity?

iBone

Price: £1.99 / $2.49
Developed By: Spoonjack
In-app Purchases: Yes (additional songs)

Thanks to iBone, all kinds of instruments get a digital makeover on the iPad from the harp to the titular trombone. Using your fingers on the screen or blowing on the microphone to make a sound, you can then slide your finger to change the pitch and volume. What's more, you can also play along with your new digital instruments to any tracks in your iTunes collection or even download trombone tracks to toot in time with.

Loop Twister

Price: £0.69 / $0.99
Developed By: Waveforms
In-app Purchases: No

While apps like Garageband come pre-loaded with their own loops amid all the other instruments, Loop Twister is a dedicated musical loop app designed to help you create and process your own sounds. It comes packed with 64 different loops created by Marcin Cichy (from the infamous Ninja Tune label), as well as allowing you to import your own loops before using a selection of filters and faders to mess with them.

AmpKit+

Price: £13.99 / $19.99
Developed By: Agile Partners
In-app Purchases: Yes (more pedals, amp styles)

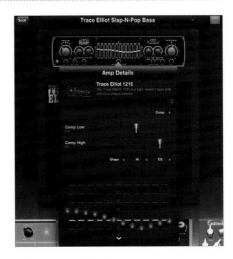

We know exactly what you're thinking, you know: you're sitting there, looking at the information above and wondering "How much!?" in a very loud inner voice. And, to be fair, you're right: AmpKit+ is one of the most expensive apps we've ever seen (excluding scam apps, that is) and it only gets more expensive once you start throwing in a couple of extra pounds each for additional pedals or a whopping £14 more for packages of six new amps and eight new pedals. But you know what? Music's a serious business and if you want the best, you need to invest.

The fact is AmpKit+ is as close as you're going to get to owning an amp without actually owning an amp. Offering both guitar and bass settings with 36 amp channels, 24 effects, 21 cabinets, 114 different presets and eight mics as standard, you can plug your guitar straight into your iPad and jam away as though you were plugged into the real thing. Of course, the app then takes things one step further by offering the ability to record your efforts and mix them down, as well as supporting background audio as well for the perfect session. Throw in all the different pedals that you can get as in-app purchases (from D-Delay and acoustic to the essential Wahba Doo pedal) and you have an entire creative suite for your guitar in a single package.

Beatwave

Price: Free
Developed By: Collect3
In-app Purchases: Yes (instrument packs)

Standing in for the iPhone-only Bloom app, Beatwave does a similar trick with its extreme psychedelic creativity, but with a more dance-style, regimented feel to it. By touching the coloured blobs on screen, you can create different sounds; tap a range of blobs and you get a tune (or what's meant to resemble one, if you do it randomly). You can assign instruments and change the tempo or tone, as well as create multiple patterns for rhythmic beats. With multiple layers, you can create a four-track piece of music or samples that can saved. There's also the ability to purchase in-app sound packs and to upgrade to a Pro version, which comes with even more features.

Last.fm

Price: Free
Developed By: Last.Fm
In-app Purchases: Yes (Pro upgrade)

Last.fm does two things very well: it lets you listen to music and it lets you keep track of what music you've listened to. If you don't want to pay to use it on your iPad, you can only use its tracking facilities, which will log every song you listen to and produce live data on your most listened artists, albums and songs. If, however, you actually want to stream some music, you'll need to sign up for a £3 per month subscription, which lets you use Last.fm like your own personal radio station. Based on the music it knows you like and what other users with similar tastes are also into, it can create endless personalised playlists that might just introduce you to your new favourite band.

Cleartune

Price: £2.49 / $3.99
Developed By: Bitcloud Ltd
In-app Purchases: No

You know what a chromatic tuner is, right? It's one of those things that lets you tune an instrument to the right pitch, allowing for the best sound possible. Not surprisingly, Cleartune is the app equivalent of the real thing and, as you should be able to tell by the quotes from famous musicians scattered all over the App Store page, it works incredibly well. It has everything a serious musician needs to get their instruments in gear, from fine tuning settings to tone waveforms and all kinds of other things that we won't pretend to understand. It runs off the microphone of your iPad too, so you don't even need any expensive connectors to make it work properly.

KORG iKaossilator

Price: £13.99 / $19.99
Developed By: Korg
In-app Purchases: Yes (samples)

Known as a giant in the synthesiser world, it's no surprise that Korg brings a suitably monster product to the iPad (both in terms of what it can do and the rather sizable price attached to it). Pitched at both experts and non-musicians, it lets the user's touch help to create music, with taps, rubs and strokes, creating a sound space with a massive range of effects.

There are 150 built-in sounds and a range of key and scale settings – along with a five-part loop sequencer to feed loops into – to create an overall tune with export mode to save your creations as regular tracks. The iKaossilator app also uses an X and Y graph interface to help create melodies and phrases just through finger strokes on the screen. Its smart display makes it feel less like music creation and more like a game, but the effects are powerful and professional.

The loop sequencer lets you layer up to five distinct pieces to create a track that can have either synthesiser, bass, chords, sound effects or drums. It can also be used in live performances to jazz up whatever you're playing to a party or crowd. Sure, it's pricey, but for a ridiculously powerful music creator that's simple to use, it's definitely worth it.

Alchemy Synth Mobile

Price: Free
Developed By: Camel Audio
In-app Purchases: Yes (Pro upgrade)

The free version of Alchemy Synth still has a good array of features, only lacking the export, load and save facilities of the in-app purchase Pro version (which is £10.49, if you feel that you have to upgrade for the added bits). You get a remix pad to morph to create your own sound effects, and a range of performance controls so you can easily tweak sounds to fit your music. There's also a loop player with 25 drum loops included (with copy and paste to use loops from other apps for use in Alchemy) with a velocity-sensitive keyboard, sound sliders and touch squares to alter the effects and more to help you decide if you want the full app or not.

Synth

Price: Free
Developed By: Retronyms
In-app Purchases: Yes (parameter editor)

Yet another polyphonic synthesiser app for the iPad, but this one comes with the added endorsement from The Gorillaz, who apparently used Synth on their last album. Whether that's enough of a reason to get hold of it is your call, but the fact that it's free and comes with over 40 different instruments, a variety of modification and pitch/bend settings, delay, distortion and the ability to plug in your own microphone to record your own samples should also go some way to persuading you. True, you'll need to make a few in-app purchases to the tune of £6 in order to unlock its full potential, but that's still a damn sight less than it'd cost to buy a proper synth...

Shazam For iPad

Price: Free
Developed By: Shazam
In-app Purchases: Yes (iTunes downloads)

As music apps go, Shazam is a classic and one of the most downloaded ever on the App Store, thanks to its ability to help anyone hearing a song that they can't identify. Not only can the app name the song just by hearing a snippet of it, but it can provide the lyrics in time to the music, offer links to music videos of that song and even let you buy the song off iTunes if it's in the archive.

Highly accurate to a scary degree, you can tag songs you discover via the app and share them with friends and get more information on the artist. Wherever you are, if you hear a song you like but don't know, Shazam is the app to help you find out more about it.

iTip – OTHER APP RECOMMENDATIONS
You might also like to try InstanTune (69p/99c) to create your own playlists and Name This (Free), a classic music quiz testing your knowledge on the last five decades.

Fireworks

Price: £0.69 / $0.99
Developed By: Computer Docs
In-In-app Purchases: No

Rather than just play pretty visualisers based on your music like many other music-reaction apps do, Fireworks instead lets you create your own show-off display with whizz bangs, explosions and sparks. These effects can be set against a backdrop of your choosing with a range of added filters, and it can play some optional sound effects to jazz up a tune if it's a bit boring.

Songbird.me

Price: Free
Developed By: Songbird
In-app Purchases: No

Get all the latest info on your favourite artists with this handy app. Tell it who you want to know about and it pulls in real-time updates to let you know what they're up to, whether that's announcing a new tour or releasing a new single. You can also share your own photos and fan art with other users, find out about new bands you might like, and even make new friends based on music tastes.

myDrum Pad

Price: £2.99 / $4.99
Developed By: Decaf Ninja
In-app Purchases: Yes (sound packs)

As you might have guessed from the name, myDrum Pad is a multi-touch drum pad app that lets you play beats, drums, hi-hats, guitar strums and other sounds to make your own music. With a smart-looking design and recording functions, you can create multiple pads and jam to your heart's content without the need for a space-hogging drum kit and the ensuing racket.

TNRi

Price: £13.99 / $19.99
Developed By: Yamaha
In-app Purchases: No

Using a simple grid made up of many different selectable dots, Yamaha's TNRi synth app is actually based on a real piece of hardware (even though it looks like a child's toy), but works just as well on the iPad. Tap the spots to create a sound, with up to six layers of music in a composition and different modes for new effects. The included demo mode lets you try everything out first, so you don't have to shell out ahead of time.

Pro Metronome

Price: Free
Developed By: Xiao Yixiang
In-app Purchases: No

A metronome might sound like a boring kind of accessory, but they can be absolutely essential if you're planning to play music alongside other people. This app lets you set any time signature you want and then keeps time for you in whichever way is most useful to you. There are seven different metronome tones, or, if you need it to be quiet, you can set it to flash or vibrate on the beat instead. Simple, easy and it does the job.

Lucky Voice Karaoke

Price: Free
Developed By: Lucky Voice Group
In-app Purchases: Yes (song credits)

If you've never heard of Lucky Voice, it's a chain of famous karaoke lounges in London. However, the Lucky Voice app brings the same karaoke experience into your lounge instead. Pay for song credits (just as you'd pay for time in the real LV) and then stream songs and their lyrics to your iPad to sing along to. You can also use Airplay to mirror output to a TV and have everyone join in. Just £58 for a full year's subscription? Bargain!

iPad mini

Your iPad mini And...
Gaming

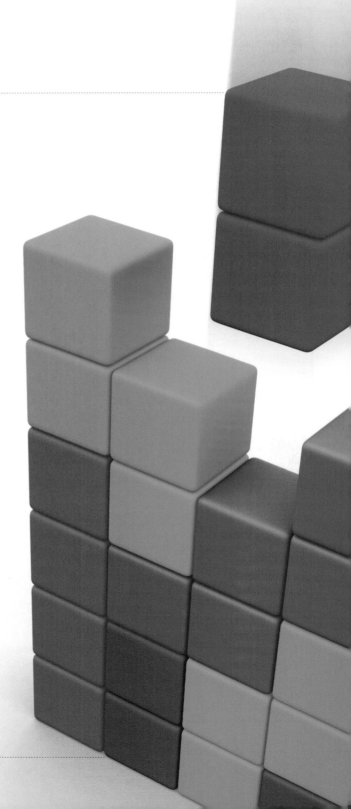

Back when Apple first envisaged and launched the iPad, gaming wasn't anywhere near the top of its agenda. It didn't think it was taking on the Nintendos and the PlayStations of the world. The iPad was, after all, a device where music and video were given a higher priority at first (unsurprising, given the massive success of the iPod and iPhone), as portable gaming was more than adequately catered for by the likes of Nintendo and its DS range of handheld consoles.

It's interesting, though, how things have panned out. As things stand now, it's Nintendo that's lost some of its footing, as it struggles to enjoy the same level of success for its handheld games machines that it once did. Instead, more and more game developers have taken to the iPad as the marketplace of choice for their wares, generating an abundance of titles, both free and paid for. It's meant that the App Store itself has become as big a games retailer as you'll find anywhere on the planet, as titles such as *Angry Birds*, *Scrabble*, *Words With Friends* and *Bejeweled* are being downloaded at a rate of knots.

Dig deeper, though, and you'll find yet more cracking titles, which make terrific use of the iPad mini's touch-screen interface. Granted, things tend to be weighted more towards puzzle games and word titles, but there's a surprising mix, and the vast majority are very, very keenly priced.

What's more, there's a burgeoning independent gaming scene, with talented programmers coming up with titles that take on much bigger companies, and still manage to prevail. This means that each and every day, there's another host of new, keenly-priced titles heading to the App Store. Do note that some, while free, are very clever at stinging you with in-app purchases though, once you've become addicted to the title in question.

So let's take you on a guided tour of some of the best games available for your iPad mini. You might just want to put aside the rest of the day too, if you're planning on downloading any of them. To say that some of these are quite addictive would be no understatement whatsoever...

82 The Best Games For iPad

- Beat Sneak Bandit
- Magnetic Billiards: Blueprint
- Coaster Crazy
- Bumpy Road
- Agent Dash
- SpellTower
- Robot Unicorn Attack
- Infinity Blade II
- Pix'n Love Rush DX
- Quarrel Deluxe
- Jazz: Trump's Journey
- Bejeweled Blitz
- World Of Goo HD

- Groove Coaster
- Angry Birds
- Draw Something
- Assassin's Creed: Recollection
- Burnout CRASH!
- Hero Academy
- Symphonica
- Words With Friends HD
- Tiny Tower
- Bag It! HD
- Incoboto
- SongPop
- Radballs
- Jetpack Joyride
- DrawRace 2
- Fibble HD
- Doors&Rooms
- Dream Of Pixels
- Match Panic
- Feed Me Oil HD
- Ticket To Ride
- Drop7
- LostWinds
- FlickPig
- Superbrothers: Sword And Sworcery EP
- Shantae: Risky's Revenge

Beat Sneak Bandit

Price: £1.99 / $2.99
Developed By: Simogo
In-app Purchases: No

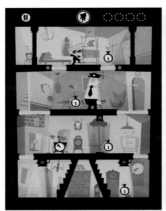
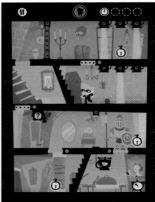

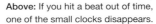

Above: If you hit a beat out of time, one of the small clocks disappears.

Above: Trapdoors open and shut, lights blink on and off…

Swedish duo Simogo follows the lazy Sunday trip of *Bumpy Road* with a faster-paced foot-tapper, expertly mixing stealth and funky grooves in the best rhythm-action game on the App Store to date

Many iOS developers stick to what they know. Just ask the storytellers at Kairosoft that seem to put out the same game with a different skin every week. Simogo, however, is different. While *Bumpy Road* (which is so great, we've reviewed it across the page) was a gentle journey down memory lane in an autumnal patchwork setting, follow-up *Beat Sneak Bandit* introduces its bright, angular cartoon world in rhythmic fashion, sliding four strips onto the screen to a metronomic beat. The cartoon visuals might be similarly appealing, but the style is very different indeed.

And if the setting strikes you as new, then the mechanics will seem even fresher. You play the bandit thief of the title, with your job being to sneak around the mansion home of Duke Clockface, who has rather bizarrely decided to steal all the clocks in the world. Why? That's for you to find out, and in true puzzle game fashion, the stolen timepieces are scattered across various rooms: there are four smaller 'bonus' clocks in each and one larger one. Pick that up and the level ends immediately.

It isn't quite that simple, of course. Everything within the mansion runs to a strict 4/4 beat, and if you move too early or too late, one of the smaller clocks located on the same floor that you're standing on (and occasionally above or below you) will vanish. Movement is, thankfully, very simple: tapping the screen sends the bandit forward one space, whether it's along the same floor or up a ladder to the next, and turns him around when he reaches a wall. You'll need to walk over retractable platforms when they click into place or drop through to the floor below when they slide back. Figuring out the route that will take you through all four smaller clocks on the way to the big one is all part of the fun, especially since you need to think your way around the rules. For instance, you'll always go up stairs when you're facing them; there's no way to go round unless you're coming from the other side.

Then there are the hazards to consider. Security guards follow a straightforward patrol route and you'll have to wait until their backs are turned or stun them by stepping on their head as they pass underneath a hole in the floor. Hovering 'vacuum busters'

will edge towards you with every beat, sucking you up if they reach your position, and security-summoning searchlights flick on and off. By the third set of stages, you'll also have teleporters to deal with, while the final collection of levels introduce time-halting switches that force you to race into position as quickly as possible before everything returns to normal.

The 40 main stages can be completed without too much trouble, but nabbing all the clocks is a seriously tricky ask on some stages, forcing you to take circuitous routes with immaculate timing to grab them. It's worth the effort too, because grabbing enough small clocks in a set of stages unlocks a number of silhouetted shadow levels, set to a jazz piano backing, which represents a surprising – yet welcome - departure from the catchy funk numbers that soundtrack the rest of the game. It all ends with an ingenious boss fight that tests your beat-matching capacity to its fullest, followed by a post-game treat or reworked stages with extra difficulty to keep you playing even longer than you would have done normally.

The beauty of *Beat Sneak Bandit* is that everything slots together with the same mechanical precision of the doors, floors and traps in Duke Clockface's mansion. Everything moves to a predictable pattern and picking out the individual rhythms of the accompanying sound effects carries the same satisfaction as solving a particularly challenging puzzle. The pacing, too, is immaculate, with some stages forcing a sprint finish, while others require you to wait it out before advancing. That it's all brought together with such a characterful art style and mind-invadingly catchy music is the icing on the cake.

It is, in short, one of the most polished, finely tuned and beautifully constructed games on iOS - a triumphant genre-bending hit. Goodness only knows how Simogo plans to top this, but one thing's for certain: we're looking forward to seeing it try in the near future…

Magnetic Billiards: Blueprint

Price: Free
Developed By: Zee-3
In-app Purchases: Yes (levels, minigames, skeleton key)

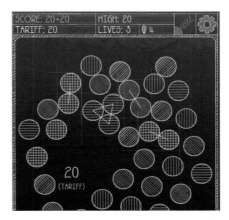

From game design veterans The Pickford Bros comes this wonderfully eccentric title that blends puzzle games with ball sports to great effect. Although the inclusion of billiards in the title might suggest otherwise, your job isn't to pot the balls but to fire them into groups of four or more to remove them from play. To maximize your score you'll need to pull off trick shots that bounce off walls around the table, building your combo by narrowly missing other balls and then landing clusters of specific shapes.

It may seem confusing at first (although the built-in tutorial is well laid out and pretty self-explanatory), but after a while the mechanics will become second nature and you'll soon be racking up the S-ranks. Then you'll unlock the Serious tables, which is where the real challenge begins.

As if those weren't enough, there are also several further variant modes that require almost the exact opposite approach, as you endeavour to clear the table quickly before it becomes too crowded due to new balls appearing after every turn you take.

What sets *Magnetic Billiards: Blueprint* apart from the myriad puzzle games on the App Store, however, is its rare level of polish and warm sense of humour, with cartoon effigies of the Pickfords and the boys themselves shouting "Marvellous!" after particularly skilful shots - although they could just as easily be describing the game itself.

Coaster Crazy

Price: Free
Developed By: Frontier Developments
In-app Purchases: Yes (Coins etc)

Ever wanted to build your own rollercoaster? Coaster Crazy casts you as a theme park developer. The crazies are ride fanatics, and in order to earn money and experience points, you'll need to build increasingly elaborate rollercoasters that meet all of their requirements. The more successful you are, the more theme parks you get to open, as the game lets you move around the world, building ever faster, scarier, and more thrilling rides as you go. The graphics are cute and cartoony, and since the crazies are invincible, it won't matter if your rollercoaster isn't quite complete when you send them off for a test drive. Oh, and then there are the zombies...

Bumpy Road

Price: £1.99 / $2.99
Developed By: Simogo
In-app Purchases: No

Scandinavian developer Simogo (developer of *Beat Sneak Bandit*, which we've reviewed on the left) takes us on a gentle Sunday drive with an elderly couple who pootle around in their dinky car, collecting various trinkets and photographs as they reminisce about their past. It might sound awfully twee but it's actually rather touching, both figuratively and literally: you guide the car using your finger to raise and lower the road underneath your car which, as befitting a surface more akin to the keys of a xylophone than a strip of tarmac, plays musical notes as you touch it. Beautiful, whimsical and totally moving, it's a true iOS original.

Agent Dash

Price: Free
Developed By: Full Fat
In-app Purchases: Yes

Game developer Full Fat is best known for its sports games, which include *Flick Soccer* and *NFL Flick Quarterback,* but it also ventures into other genres, like this lightning-paced running game. *Agent Dash* might be the world's fastest secret agent: his mission is to destroy supervillains' bases, dodging obstacles and grabbing jetpacks and other handy tools along the way. Since supervillains tend to want to defend their top-secret hideaways, you'll have to navigate all sorts of perils, facing everything from boiling lava to lethal laser beams. You probably won't want to play it for hours on end, but it's fun enough to dip in and out of, and the slick graphics set it apart from other games in the same vein.

iPad mini

83

SpellTower

Price: £1.49 / $1.99
Developed By: Zach Gage
In-app Purchases: No

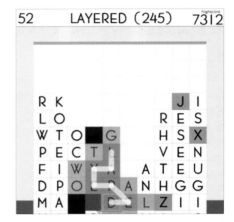

It's rare that you'll hear an iOS game described as 'classy', but Zach Gage's brilliant word game can't be considered as anything else. It may be little more than a word search grid with bells on, but such is the simplicity and beauty of its user interface that it's an absolute joy to play with.

After a wonderfully brisk tutorial that takes you through the basics, the default Tower mode asks you to amass as high a score as possible from a grid containing 100 letters. To do so, you simply trace your finger over adjacent tiles to form words. Interestingly, you can move in any direction including diagonals to do this, even moving backwards in some cases. Complete a word and the tiles disappear, allowing the tiles above to drop into the gap it leaves, while words with blue letters in clear away an entire row of tiles when removed.

That's the simplest mode, but the other game types are much more stressful. Puzzle Mode adds a new row for each word you make, as you try not to let any columns reach the top of the screen. Rush mode is similar in design but adds a fairly tight time limit into the mix, forcing you to think fast. With some tiles enforcing a minimum word length before you can clear them away, the challenge soon ramps up, and consistently locating five-letter words under pressure can be surprisingly tricky. However, this never once proves frustrating and is instead a real joy to play from start to finish.

Robot Unicorn Attack

Price: £0.69 / $0.99
Developed By: Adult Swim
In-app Purchases: No

How much you're going to love this game depends entirely on how appealing you find the prospect of playing a rainbow-spouting robot unicorn running across an endless landscape while Erasure's 'Always' plays on loop, because that's really all there is to the game. You control the unicorn's speed and jumps, and it just keeps going until you're not quick enough to avoid one of the game's many pitfalls. It's really, really silly, but somehow really, really addictive too. Adult Swim's games are all gorgeous to look at and this is no exception, provided you're into bright colours. It might not require much brainpower to play, but it's utterly absorbing nonetheless.

Infinity Blade II

Price: £4.99 / $6.99
Developed By: Chair Entertainment
In-app Purchases: Yes (additional gold)

Arguably the most technically accomplished game on the App Store and one of the few games that's really been beefed up to take advantage of the new iPad's graphical power, *Chair*'s sequel revisits the *Punch Out*-meets-*Rogue*-like approach of its predecessor, but with much greater combat variety and even more detailed graphics. At times, when the screen fills with flesh and armour and you're swiping away wildly, it can still feel a little like slicing huge chunks of meat wrapped in tinfoil. However, its structure constantly encourages you to have just one more battle; when you look up and realise it's 2am, you'll know you're hooked all over again.

Pix'n Love Rush DX

Price: £1.99 / $2.99
Developed By: Pastagames
In-app Purchases: No

A charming blend of the endless runner genre that's become popular on iOS devices and an old-school platformer from the days of the SNES, this bright, happy and instantly compelling game sees you control a wonky-eyed pixel cat through a series of simple game modes. Although many retro-themed titles suffer without actual buttons to guide the action, *Pix'n Love Rush DX*'s controls are perfectly calibrated as you dash, jump and dodge across its stylised stages. With a chiptune soundtrack burbling away merrily throughout, it's both a reminder of a simpler time and further proof that the Apple's devices are the new home of the classic arcade game.

Quarrel Deluxe

Price: £1.99 / $2.99
Developed By: Denki
In-app Purchases: No

'It's Risk meets Scrabble' is the simplest way to describe *Quarrel DX*, but in many ways it's also the most accurate since that's basically what it is. Taken as a whole, it's a battle for word domination as you attempt to control all territories on a board by scoring more highly than the opponents defending their turf. Not surprisingly, though, it's a little more complicated than just coming up with the longest word you can think of.

Each skirmish that you undertake sparks a timed word game. You're given eight letters from which you must find a high-scoring word before the clock runs down. Emerge with a higher tally than your rival or beat them to the punch with an identical score and the land is yours. The trouble is the number of letters you have to play with depends on the number of troops accompanying you on each sortie, so you have to make the highest-scoring word with a set number of letters. With your army dwindling after every move (then topped up after you've finished your turn), you have to decide whether to risk facing an opponent with a lesser force or to play tactically and leave men back to defend your own areas of control safely.

It's a shame it lacks a multiplayer mode, but *Quarrel Deluxe* offers plenty of challenge for the lone player, with AI rivals whose unique behaviour makes a convincing stand-in for human opponents. Some are word kings but strategic dunces, others play more cautiously, and then there's Kali... Charming and clever, it's quite simply another Denki classic.

Jazz: Trump's Journey

Price: £1.99 / $2.99
Developed By: Bulkypix
In-app Purchases: No

Believe it or not, this funky little platformer is actually based on the real life story of Louis Armstrong (although we doubt he had to jump over platforms). You play as titular trumpet player Trump, guiding him through New Orleans as he collects musical notes and band members so he can put on a jazz show to make his grandma proud. Platformers don't always work on iOS, but the controls here are well-judged and a gentle but still challenging puzzle element comes into play once you discover that Trump's instrument can manipulate time. Its riddles may be familiar, but its setting is delightful and the wonderful soundtrack enhances a charming adventure.

Bejeweled Blitz

Price: Free
Developed By: PopCap
In-app Purchases: Yes (coins)

Bejeweled is a classic by anyone's standards. All you have to do is rearrange jewels in a giant grid so that three or more of the same type are lined up in a row, at which point they'll disappear and be replaced with more. This version adds power-ups and special rewards for achieving certain combinations, but the gameplay is essentially the same. On the iPad, you move jewels by swiping them with your finger. This might have been a bit fiddly on the iPhone, but on the iPad screen it's very simple, and the jewels look great on the Retina Display. It might not be sophisticated, but some games are iconic for a reason, and once you start playing this, you'll find it hard to stop.

World Of Goo HD

Price: £1.99 / $2.99
Developed By: 2D Boy
In-app Purchases: No

2D Boy's cult PC and WiiWare classic has finally found its true home on Apple's iOS devices. That's not just because the price makes it accessible to those who don't like spending money on games, but because the touch interface proves a revelation for the physics-based conundrums here as you build elaborate constructions to guide the titular goo (represented by a series of cute blobs) towards the exit pipe. There's a wonderful illusion of elasticity that's only enhanced by using your fingers directly rather than a mouse or remote pointer to stretch the different types of blobs into position, making the iOS version the definitive take on an already immaculate puzzle game.

Groove Coaster

Price: £1.99 / $2.99
Developed By: Taito
In-app Purchases: Yes (extra music tracks)

Reisuke Ishida is fast becoming one of Taito's most important development assets. Having already created *Space Invaders Infinity Gene* – a remake of the classic *Space Invaders* that combines music and power-ups with the retro gameplay of its namesake – he goes one better with this psychedelic rhythm-action game that tests your reflexes and memory as much as it does your beat-matching capabilities.

The idea is to tap the screen as your avatar passes touch points along a set track that curves, plunges and zigzags in time with the background music. You'll hit percussive beats and then melodic tones as you switch between instruments automatically and seamlessly, the game testing your ability to recognise a variety of rhythms within the same song.

At other times you'll need to scratch left and right for a time, hold your finger down or keep tapping for the duration of a sustained note. It might sound simple, but the tracks move at a heck of a pace, with frequent perspective shifts and the neon-lit visuals along the way proving quite disorientating.

The tracklist is thrillingly varied, taking in jazz-tinged numbers, scuzzy guitar licks and thudding techno, while an RPG-esque levelling mechanic opens up new skins, avatars and other power-ups. It's just a shame about all the in-app purchases that tempt you to spend more money with things like new music tracks and consumable items that don't do much, but hey...

Angry Birds

Price: £0.69 / $0.99
Developed By: Rovio Entertainment
In-app Purchases: Yes (upgrades, etc)

Angry Birds is so popular you'd almost think it came pre-installed on every Apple device. It's a simple game of projectile weapons and easily collapsible castles. You control the birds, who are angry because the evil green pigs have stolen their eggs. Launching the birds into the pigs' castles knocks everything over and wins you your eggs back, but as soon as you knock one castle down, the pigs have built another one... Each type of bird has a different ability, which mixes things up a bit, and it's just ridiculously addictive. Once you've finished this game, there's a world of further variations, including *Star Wars Angry Birds* and even a pigs spin-off, *Bad Piggies...*

Draw Something

Price: £1.99 / $2.99
Developed By: OMGPop
In-app Purchases: Yes (coins)

Create an artistic masterpiece using your iPad as your canvas, and then watch in horror as your opponent guesses the word you're drawing within seconds. *Draw Something* is basically like Pictionary, if you were allowed tons of different colours and plenty of time to play - and if you could play it against people on the other side of the world, of course! It's pretty straightforward. The game gives you a choice of words, you pick one and attempt to draw something that'll allow your opponent to guess the word. You both get coins if you can successfully communicate, and coins mean you can unlock more colours, or special sets of words.

Assassin's Creed: Recollection

Price: Free
Developed By: Ubisoft
In-app Purchases: Yes (credits)

Ignore the incredibly attractive price that Recollection offers: you'll still need to spend a fair bit of money to be genuinely competitive in this online/offline multiplayer card game, and it'll take plenty of time to master its complexities (though *Magic: The Gathering* fans will be on familiar ground). The investment in both cases is well worth it, though, as this is a deck-building game with real depth, crafted with attention to detail and enviable polish. The real-time setup adds a note of urgency to contests, and it's both flexible and accessible, with thorough tutorials and a surprisingly gentle learning curve.

Burnout CRASH!

Price: £2.99/ $4.99
Developed By: Criterion Games
In-In-app Purchases: No

Criterion's fender-bending downloadable console hit finally arrives on the App Store with a fresh lick of paint, and it proves even more dangerously addictive than ever in its natural habitat.

There really wasn't an awful lot wrong with *Burnout CRASH!*'s debut on Xbox Live Arcade; it merely felt like a game on the wrong format. Those who had been hoping for a new *Burnout* in the style of previous entries in Criterion's raucous racing series were left disappointed by a top-down casual-friendly party game that seemed like an iOS title inexplicably blown up for the big screen. Now, though, it's finally arrived on the format that it originally seemed to be made for, and it's a perfect fit.

The objective remains the same as it did before: you steer your vehicle into a junction and attempt to annihilate as many automobiles as you can, though Criterion has made a few changes to the formula in preparation for its new home. The structure has been tweaked for starters: the divisive Road Block game mode, which players had to complete before others were unlocked is now third on the list rather than first, though the three modes can be played in any order.

It seems the difficulty has been tweaked too, although perhaps that's partly down to the touch controls, which make flinging your car about easier and more intuitive than ever. Hitting a single car gradually increases your Crashbreaker meter and when filled you can trigger an explosion, swiping to manoeuvre your vehicle to cause as much damage as possible. Even when the meter is empty, you can bunny-hop closer to your chosen target.

The upshot is that Road Block instantly becomes much more enjoyable. While you're still tasked with preventing five cars from passing through the junction unscathed, it's far simpler to obstruct their exit and thus build your way up to the special features that really help rack up the points. Hit a pizza van and you'll be asked to spin a wheel for a random bonus, while letting an ambulance pass to safety removes a single cross from your tally of escapee vehicles. Nabbing a magnet attracts all vehicles to your location, allowing you to create chain reactions and earn skill shot bonuses, while pushing other cars into sinkholes nets you further cash.

Last long enough and you'll earn that area's super feature: these range from plane crashes to tornadoes to tsunamis and

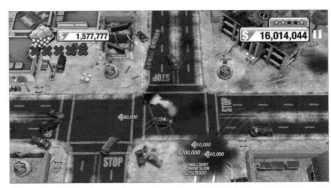
Above: As the junctions get more complex, so do the tactics needed to win.

Above: Aliens! Everybody run! Or, rather, everybody get blown to pieces!

even flying saucers, and they will usually net you the star for passing the final points tally for that stage. There are five stars to earn for each junction, and these unlock new levels and additional vehicles to play around with.

Pile Up mode isn't quite as much fun, asking you to crash a certain number of cars before burning them up for big bucks. Instead, Rush Hour is the real winner, giving you a full 90 seconds to wreak all kinds of havoc without fear of penalty.

It's this mode you'll likely return to for high-score attempts, and EA's Autolog allows you to view and compete against your friends' totals as you battle for leaderboard supremacy. It does require you to sign up to the publisher's Origin service, but it's worth it, because it's here that the real longevity lies once you've conquered all the junctions in your favourite modes.

Thankfully, *Burnout CRASH!* remains as gaudy, brash and silly as it was on its XBLA debut. This is a game where Spandau Ballet's 'Gold' plays when you hit a glittering car, where Gloria Estefan's 'Dr. Beat' heralds an ambulance's arrival and where Shirley Bassey sings when a bank van goes boom. It's bright, fun and wonderfully cathartic, and it's accessible to players of all skill levels.

Anyone with an appetite for iOS destruction should race onto the App Store and download it now.

iPad mini

Hero Academy

Price: Free
Developed By: Robot Entertainment
In-app Purchases: Yes (teams, colours, avatars)

Developer Robot Entertainment's staff has plenty of tactical nous, with the likes of *Age of Empires* and *Halo Wars* on their CVs. It shows in this multiplayer-only turn-based strategy, albeit one that reverses an iOS standard: instead of collecting gems, your objective is to smash them.

The alternative to destroying your rival's crystals is to annihilate the enemy to win, though the violence here is gentle and cartoonish as fantasy archetypes battle it out on a series of rudimentary 9x5 grids. The characters might be clichéd, but they're well-drawn and designed in a way that makes their type (healer, mage, warrior) instantly obvious.

Each player has five moves per turn, which is sufficient to accomplish certain tasks (form a defensive perimeter, defeat a single enemy) but never enough to cover every eventuality that your opponent can cook up. In addition to moving or attacking,

you can also apply defensive or offensive buffs, cast area-of-effect spells or revive fallen troops.

Even with a variety of very different teams (the Council can be used on the free download, but you'll have to pay for the Dark Elves, the Dwarves and the Tribe), it's a well-balanced effort, and the interface is so crisp it could easily be called Hero Academy With Friends. Thank goodness Zygna hasn't got it yet...

Symphonica

Price: Free
Developed By: Square Enix
In-app Purchases: More episodes

Help wannabe conductor Takt fulfill his dreams in this anime-style music game. You'll need to make sure your orchestra is under control and sounding great in order to progress. There are about 50 different pieces of classical music built into the game, and you'll need to master them all to succeed. Unlike *Rock Band* or other music games, you can't pick and choose here; the music is part of the story, and you'll need to play your way through each piece in turn if you want to succeed. It's not the most obvious profession to make a game about, but conducting is more difficult than it looks, and you'll gain a new appreciation for that through playing *Symphonica*. Plus it looks gorgeous.

Words With Friends HD

Price: £1.99/ $2.99
Developed By: Zynga Mobile
In-app Purchases: Yes (tokens)

It's Scrabble by any other name, although saying that would probably have a whole heap of copyright lawyers on your back. Produced in response to a lack of online multiplayer in the officially licensed Electronic Arts app, *Words With Friends* managed to steal the thunder of Hasbro's game by allowing users to connect to friends and random opponents anywhere in the world. It plays pretty much identically to the word game you all know and love, but it benefits enormously from a clear, readable, user-friendly interface and sensible options, even down to the ability to simply shake to rearrange your tiles. Little wonder it's one of the most popular word games on iOS...

Tiny Tower

Price: Free
Developed By: NimbleBit
In-app Purchases: Yes (Tower 'Bux')

Running laundromats, arcades, cake shops and sushi bars, the 'bitizens' of *Tiny Tower* are a busy bunch and it's up to you to help make their businesses a success by bowing to their every whim. You'll need to match their abilities to an appropriate role, ensure products are regularly stocked and ferry non-workers about using your finger to guide the elevator. You're essentially doing fairly menial tasks that all amount to pressing buttons over and over again, but that won't stop you from picking up your phone every ten minutes to see how your pixelated people are getting along. It's worryingly addictive stuff, especially since the new mission elements were added.

Bag It! HD

Price: £1.99 / $2.99
Developed By: Hidden Variable Studios
In-app Purchases: Yes (mode unlocks)

'Tetris in a shopping bag' was probably the pitch for this inventive puzzle game. However, if it started with similar intentions, Hidden Variable Studios has worked wonders in revising the formula across a series of modes where you'll constantly need to reassess your strategy.

At its core, it's all about adjusting the position of items in your shopping bag to make them all fit without crushing any breakables. That's easier said than done: once you've taken an item from the conveyor belt, you're committed to slotting it in place. You're limited to the space within the bag, so smaller objects like orange juice cartons can be more easily manipulated than the hefty watermelons, while fragile egg boxes need to be handled with care.

Star ratings are gained for reaching certain points tallies, for filling the bag to a certain percentage (with bonus points for packing as tightly as possible) or for placing certain items next to each other to create combos (for instance, placing three packets of nacho chips side by side to make a 'Three Amigos' set). Secret objectives award silver and gold medals, also unlocking stages ranging from puzzle challenges where you're not allowed to break a single item, to a mode that asks you to bag up items as quickly as possible before they're destroyed by a rogue barcode scanner.

Incoboto

Price: £2.49 / $3.99
Developed By: Fluttermind
In-app Purchases: No

This charmingly elegant puzzle-platformer is the brainchild of Dene Carter, co-creator of the *Fable* series. Not surprisingly, the developer's past work is evident in what is a similarly well-crafted adventure, full of clever and darkly humorous moments. You play a diminutive astronaut, exploring an empty universe with the last remaining sun, returning light to the worlds you visit as you go. Its physics-powered and gravity-controlled conundrums are often real head-scratchers, the virtual touch controls are smartly calibrated to not annoy and the story carries more emotional weight than you might think. A real gem in every sense of the word.

SongPop

Price: £1.49 / $1.99
Developed By: FreshPlanet
In-app Purchases: Yes (credits)

Are you a music buff? Can you identify a random tune or artist more quickly than your friends? You can find out for sure with *SongPop*, a music guessing game in which being able to correctly identify a song one tenth of a second more quickly than your friend might mean the difference between winning and losing. The more games you win, the more coins you earn, and the more coins you have, the more playlists you can unlock. *SongPop* caters for all musical tastes, so if you're an expert on metal while your friends are mostly into jazz, you can pick the kind of music that will let you triumph (until they retaliate by picking something you find hard in the next round).

Radballs

Price: £1.99 / $2.99
Developed By: Glow Play
In-app Purchases: No

It may be yet another puzzler – a genre that the App Store is literally overflowing with – but *Radballs* is the game the cool kids play. Well, probably. It's an impossibly hip concoction with an aesthetic pieced together from every 80s electronica album cover ever made and pulsing techno tunes from former Nintendo composer Neil Voss. Fortunately, there's just as much substance behind the style, with a blob-matching puzzler that echoes Tetsuya Mizuguchi's equally cool creation *Lumines*. Meanwhile, the reactive soundtrack makes you feel like a DJ as you expertly scratch any matched orbs and the bar that descends with the beat to remove them.

Jetpack Joyride

Price: Free
Developed By: Halfbrick Studios
In-app Purchases: Yes (coin packs)

Halfbrick's *Fruit Ninja* follow-up sees the welcome return of *Age of Zombies* hero Barry Steakfries and a daring escape that turns into one of the most addictive pursuits on iOS…

You get the impression that Halfbrick has developed a deep understanding of what makes mobile gamers tick: immediacy and reward. The instant you tap the screen after loading up Jetpack Joyride, you'll witness Barry Steakfries – returning from previous Halfbrick game Age of Zombies – burst through the wall of a laboratory with a jetpack on his back. It's an explosive, arresting opening that has you gripped from the off.

Barry hits the ground running and it's up to you to get him as far as you can. The controls couldn't be simpler, as your finger activates the jetpack: hold it on the screen to ascend, let go to descend as you accelerate through the booby-trapped lab. You'll soar past electric barriers and spinning gates, dodge floating laser beams and avoid incoming missiles sent to stop Barry from making his escape. It's hectic, intense and, importantly, responsive.

The environments you'll hover through aren't particularly interesting (though an undercover arboretum that occasionally whizzes by is a pleasant change of scenery), but you'll be afraid to blink as you're travelling at such a pace. One lapse in concentration and you'll be fried.

What makes Jetpack Joyride so special is the way it's been put together. It's not that it looks nice (though its graphics are fluid and fun) and not that by your 15th consecutive go, the main theme will tunnel its way into your brain and stubbornly refuse to leave. No, it's compelling because unlike many endless runner games, it's not just about achieving distance. Were that its only goal, it'd be frustrating to those who find the whims of its random obstacle generation annoying; often it seems that luck as much as quick reflexes will get you the biggest distances. No, it's the mission system that makes the game. There are always bonus objectives to achieve, ranging from flying close to 20 zappers and getting a certain distance without collecting any coins to high-fiving 25 wandering scientists in one game. Completing these challenges awards stars that help you level up and access even more missions, so there's a sense that you're making progress even after a poor run. Then there's the fact that the coins feed into a system of upgrades and unlockables.

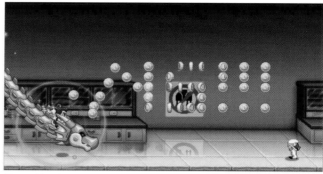

Above: Yes, the dragon's name is Mr Cuddles. No, he's not actually cuddly.

Above: The jungle environment is new, added as part of a free update.

Even if it's just to get hold of a rainbow jetpack or a new look for Barry, you'll keep coming back to grind for coins.

Then there are the vehicles. Every so often you'll find a large glowing icon that drops a mech suit, a metallic dragon or a motorbike into play, with Barry hopping on board to power forward. You can even upgrade them in the in-game shop, with magnetised vehicles instantly pulling in more money than you'd normally earn (and gold vehicles doing… well, nothing apart from proving that you've really played the game so much you have that much virtual money to burn). Even when you die, it's not always game over, because along the way, you can fly into floating spin tokens. Each one you grab enables you to spin a one-armed-bandit minigame when you die, often with the chance to resurrect yourself or be thrown that extra 100m by an explosion, perhaps helping you beat your previous best or, better still, the best scores of your friends, which are handily signposted along the way.

It's essentially a collection of perfect feedback loops. Every run, no matter how feeble, contributes to either your coin tally or your character level, encouraging further runs until you complete all the challenges – and then a new set of challenges appear. It's a game that never gets old – the main reason why it keeps us coming back for more.

DrawRace 2

Price: £1.99 / $2.99
Developed By: RedLynx
In-app Purchases: Yes (unlock keys, Supercar)

Trace a route with your finger and then sit back while you watch your car follow it: it's the kind of idea you kick yourself for not having had first and with *DrawRace 2*, RedLynx – a developer known for physics-based racers – really makes the most of it.

Realistic handling of each vehicle ensures it's not just as simple as whizzing your finger around a circuit as quickly as possible – do so and you'll hear the screech of brakes as your driver fails to take corners cleanly. Instead, you need to move your finger slower around turns to 'apply the brakes' and even consider the racing line that should be taken for each turn to be a success. Sure, it takes a while to master, but a gentle difficulty curve and some brilliant tutorial videos ease you in.

There's a wide variety of cars and tracks, with unlockables triggered for many victories (even if it's just a new challenge on an old circuit). Meanwhile, a turbo allows a risky element of real-time control after you've drawn your path – sometimes boosting you to victory, often spinning you out. It can be the difference between spoiling a perfect racing line or enhancing a tentative trace and is a terrific addition.

Additional stages ask you to pop balloons en route to the finish, while Hot Seat mode lets up to four players take it in turns to draw a path on one device. With loads of options and sublime presentation, it's the best portable racer around.

Fibble HD

Price: £2.99 / $4.99
Developed By: Crytek
In-app Purchases: Yes (unlock keys)

The first smartphone game from the maker of PC vanity shooter *Crysis* might not be quite what you're expecting from a developer with a history in first-person shooters, but this physics puzzler is typically attractive and intelligently made nevertheless. Using your finger, the aim is to ping the titular blob around obstacle courses, collecting stars on your way to the goal, with additional rewards for completing each stage in a single flick – basically crazy golf but with blobs. New abilities courtesy of Fibble's alien friends (one throws him to new heights, another can change his direction) are introduced at a sensible pace, and the difficulty curve is perfectly judged.

Doors&Rooms

Price: Free
Developed By: gameday Inc
In-app Purchases: Yes (coins)

You wake up in a room. You don't know where you are, but the door opens. Now you're in another room. This time you need to pick up a key to get out. In the next room, the challenge is more complicated. *Doors&Rooms* is a creepy little puzzle game in which you need to use everything you can possibly find in a series of almost empty rooms in order to progress to the next room. There's not much of a story, maybe (or at least not a coherent one), but the graphics are lovely and the way the game slowly trains you in how to find clues is quite smart. It's all intuitive and there's something about it that makes you want to keep going, to just see what will be in the next room.

Dream of Pixels

Price: £1.99 / $2.99
Developed By: Dawn of Play
In-app Purchases: No

Undo decades of *Tetris*-induced frustration with the lovely *Dream of Pixels*. In this game, rather than trying to make blocks fit together, you're pulling them apart, one after another. The shapes are the familiar *Tetris* configurations, but the gameplay is subtly and wonderfully different. The soft dreamy graphics are gorgeous and the music is rather soothing too. If you've ever been stuck playing *Tetris* for hours on end, to the point where you're even stacking blocks in your sleep, this might be just the remedy you need. Even if you're not, it's a lovely puzzle game anyway. It even has a Zen mode for players who want to take their time and enjoy the game without the pressure.

iPad mini

Your iPad And Gaming (continued)

iTip – OTHER APP RECOMMENDATIONS
Sword And Sworcery EP (£2.99/$4.99), an epic point-and-click adventure and Shantae: Risky's Revenge (£2.99/$4.99), a side-scrolling ninja action platformer.

Match Panic

Price: £1.49 / $1.99
Developed By: Chaotic Box
In-app Purchases: No

Pixel-art pandas, squids, stars and cacti scroll towards you along a single channel and it's your job to match them to the relevant picture on the left and right of the screen by tapping the correct side as quickly as you possibly can. It sounds absurdly simple but when there are three images per side, a stack of icons still to clear and time's running out, it's remarkably tricky to get right.

Feed Me Oil HD

Price: £1.49 / $1.99
Developed By: HolyWaterGames
In-app Purchases: Yes (instant hints)

This fluid and rather unusual physics puzzler sees you place ramps, fans, magnets and more to guide flowing streams of oil into the expectant mouths of bizarre rock monsters. It's quite fiddly but enormously satisfying; with its bizarre art style and quirky soundtrack, it's a worthy rival to World of Goo, although you're still better off getting 2D Boy's stretchy effort before this one.

Ticket To Ride

Price: £4.99 / $6.99
Developed By: Days Of Wonder
In-app Purchases: Yes (board expansions)

Almost certainly the best board game conversion available on the App Store – not to mention on of the priciest – Ticket To Ride is a clear labour of love for developer Days Of Wonder. With thorough tutorials, multiple board expansions, local multiplayer (but no online play as on the iPhone) as well as four AI rivals to compete against, there's something for every board game fan.

Drop7

Price: £1.99 / $2.99
Developed By: Zynga
In-app Purchases: No

One of the most finely tuned mind-bending concepts since Tetris powers this intelligent and incredibly compelling puzzler, as you strive to clear circular pieces by creating rows with the same number of discs as the integer on their faces. The learning curve can be steep if you don't pay attention, but stick with it through the failure and you'll soon fall under its horribly addictive spell.

LostWinds

Price: £2.49 / $3.99
Developed By: Frontier Developments
In-app Purchases: No

The downloadable WiiWare hit reaches the App Store intact, with smartly implemented touch controls that make it a breeze to control Toku and wind spirit Enril. Granted, it's rather short, but it's also an exceedingly sweet adventure, with lovely pastel-coloured settings, subtly haunting melodies and clever puzzles to bolster the engaging Metroid-like exploration throughout.

FlickPig

Price: £0.69 / $0.99
Developed By: Prope
In-app Purchases: Yes (coins)

Sonic the Hedgehog creator Yuji Naka is the brains behind this fun little curio that sees you stacking speedy swine to collect coins and avoid obstacles in a series of short, swift races. Requiring a healthy mix of strong reflexes and quick thinking, it's colourful, challenging and thoroughly entertaining – a game that both adults and children alike can pick up and play for much amusement.

Your iPad mini And...
Productivity

So far in this book, we've covered the likes of music, video and gaming on your iPad mini. However, there's a serious side too, because your tablet computer is a very capable business device too, which allows you to take your work on the move. We're talking a lot more than just e-mailing and Internet access here as well. There's effectively a portable office that you can hold in your hand.

There's a selection of software directly from Apple, for starters, which can cover the likes of word processing and spreadsheet work. We're going to take you through how to get to grips with iWork, from words and numbers, through to the impressive presentation package that's included with it. We'll go through each of these areas of the suite in detail.

Then, we're going to look at some of the many alternatives that are available in the App Store too. You don't have to use the software that Apple has provided for you if you don't want to and, in fact, there are some compelling options from other publishers.

We admit to being surprised: at first, the idea of effectively treating an iPad mini as a laptop felt just a little bit alien. However, after a little time in the company of iWork and its many alternatives, we were quickly convinced. We think you might be too.

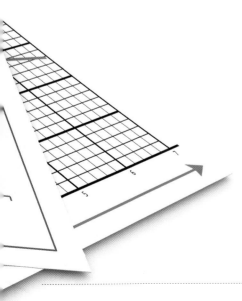

iWork

Price: £6.99 / $9.99 per app (Pages, Numbers, Keynote)
Developed By: Apple
In-app Purchases: No

Who needs to spend over £100 buying Microsoft Office on a laptop when you can spend less than £21 and get yourself an entire suit of productivity apps that'll do everything it can do, only with less fuss?

You might not know it, but Apple's had its own alternative to Microsoft Office available for a while now. Known as iWorks, the collection of three packages – Pages, Numbers and Keynote – work as perfectly serviceable and even slightly more intuitive takes on word processing, spreadsheets and presentation creation software, so it's a wonder that more people don't use them. Thanks to its iOS effectively being locked down in terms of the software that Apple allows on it, though, owners of the iPad really don't have much of a choice; it's iWorks or nothing.

Is that actually a bad thing, though? Well, no, it's not. In fact, it couldn't be further from a bad thing if it tried, since the iOS versions of Pages, Numbers and Keynote (which are universal and run on both iPad and iPhone) are both ridiculously powerful and incredibly accessible. It's almost that the idea of owning a laptop becomes null and void for the average creative type, be it for business, education or just general home tinkering with ideas.

Which one you'll want depends on what you're going to use them for, but since the apps are all available individually and priced at an insane £6.99, you can easily pick up the one you need instead of having to buy them all to access just a part of the package. What's important to realise, however, is just how much scope for creativity each app offers, despite being pigeonholed into certain genres. Granted, it's Numbers that perhaps stands as the odd one out, since it's a spreadsheet app and is thus somewhat restricted to just keeping facts and figures

in order (although there's still a huge amount you can do with it, from creating interesting and colourful reports to making 3D charts that can be altered dynamically). The other two, however, are far more than just typing and slideshows...

Take Pages, for instance: rather than being just a simple word processor, it's actually a full-on desktop publishing app. That

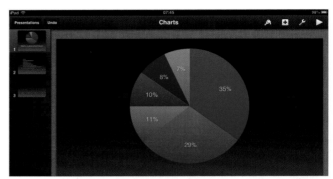

Above: Keynote can be used to create professional report-style presentations

Above: ... Or to show off a new product or toy.

means that while it can be used for simple text documents (and can even export into Word format), it's also perfect for making posters, flyers, CVs, letters, invitations and much, much more. Likewise, Keynote doesn't just have to be considered boring because it's great for making presentations; after all, who says presentations are just for business meetings? Try using it to make a slideshow of photos from your latest holiday to show your family, a moving scrapbook of memories that you can look back on whenever you're feeling sentimental or even additional education for your kids when you want to help bolster the things they're learning at school.

And while the scope is almost limitless, the means of using them are amazingly easy too. Thanks to the iPad's touch-screen, pretty much every element of iWorks is touch-based, from resizing boxes and moving pictures around a page to rotating images, copying/pasting and adjusting the angle that you view a 3D chart from. Plus, both Keynote and Pages are compatible with Dictation, meaning you don't even have to type any text to get words on the page.

We'll admit we were skeptical that iWorks would be anything more than bare-bones software when we first sat down to use it, but we've been blown away by how deep it is and how much you can do with it. And for the price each app is being sold at, it seems mad not to take Apple up on its offer...

How To Use... Keynote

You don't need to just rely on your iPad mini to show off the presentations that you make any more. Thanks to Keynote, you can use it to actually create them from scratch too

Step 1: Theming Your Presentation

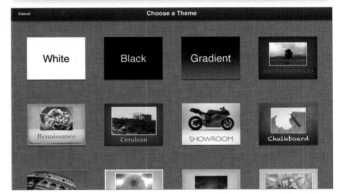

Once you've started Keynote, you'll be on the Presentation library screen that stores all your created documents for easy access. Hit the plus button in the top-left corner and choose 'Create Presentation' to start a new file, then pick a theme from the pre-loaded selection. White and Black are blank slates for you to start from, while the others have style and design created for you.

Step 2: Adding New Slides

The main editing screen of Keynote is split into the editing window, which displays each slide as it'll appear in your final presentation, and the Navigator, which shows a library of the slides you've made. Tap the plus button in the bottom-left corner to create a new slide. You'll see a selection of slide templates to choose from, although these are all totally open to editing.

How To Use... Keynote (continued)

Step 3: Altering And Adding Text

As you can probably guess, adding text onto a slide is as simple as double-tapping the text box (be it title, body, captions, whatever) and then typing away on the virtual keyboard. Keynote also works with Dictation. To select parts of the text for editing purposes, double-tap to select a specific word or triple-tap to highlight an entire paragraph of text.

Step 4: Adding And Removing Elements

While the slide templates offer a handy guide, you can alter them at will by adding more elements or deleting ones already there. To add more text or picture boxes, tap one already on the template and select 'Copy' from the option bar, then tap on a blank space of the slide and tap 'Paste' to replicate that element. To delete something, tap it and choose the 'Delete' option instead.

Step 5: Adjusting And Moving Elements

To move an element, just tap and hold on it, before dragging it into the right position. Resizing any element is done by selecting it and then dragging the blue dots around the outside in or out. If you tap another element while resizing something, Keynote will automatically resize it to match the one you touched. You can also rotate elements by touching with two fingers and twisting.

Step 6: Adding Images To A Slide

There are two ways of adding images to your slides: either import them as new elements or drop them into pre-existing picture boxes. To do the latter, just tap the box and choose 'Replace' from the options, then select the right image from your Camera Roll. To create a new image, hit the plus button in the top-right corner and select the image from your library that way instead.

iTip – BACKUP AND SHARE
As with other iWorks apps, Keynote can link to iCloud to back up and share your documents. You can turn this on/off in the 'Apps' > 'Keynote' section of Settings.

Step 5: Add Transitions

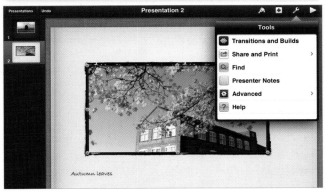

Tap the Tools (spanner) icon in the top-right corner and choose 'Transitions and Builds' to add effects to your slides. Transitions are the movement from one slide to another, such as dissolving and fading. Builds, however, relate to elements and can let you animate text boxes appearing on the page or swapping from one picture to another using the same image box on a single slide.

Step 6: Magic Move

Magic Move is an advanced transition technique; choose it and the slide you're viewing will be duplicated. Then using this duplicate, move the elements on the slide around and even add new ones. When you play the presentation, the transition between the two slides will see all the elements move around as you dictated, offering an effect that's better than a simple transition.

Step 7: Playing It Back

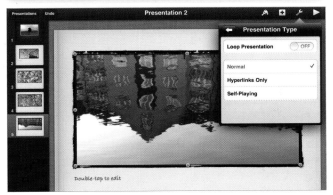

To run your presentation as a slideshow, just press the play button in the top-right corner. By default, you'll need to tap the screen to advance slides, but you can set it to run automatically in the 'Tools' > 'Advanced' > 'Presentation Type' menu. You can also set the iPad to work with an Apple Remote for moving slides forwards under the 'Advanced' > 'Remote' menu.

Step 8: Sharing And Showing Off

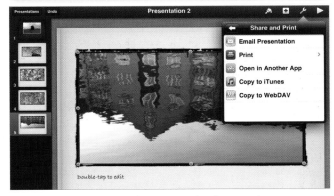

You can share your finished presentation in several ways. Obviously, you could just show it to someone on your iPad or hook it up to a TV or bigger display. You can also email your presentation, send it to a printer, copy it into your iTunes, or share it in other ways by touching the 'Share and Print' option in the Tools menu.

How To Use... Pages

Think of it as the Apple equivalent of Microsoft Word if you like, but it turns out that Pages can do a whole lot more than you'd think and with a whole lot less effort as well…

Step 1: Creating A New Document

When you first start Pages, you'll be sent to the Documents screen, which will be empty initially but as you start creating new files, they'll appear here for easy access. Tap the plus button in the top left and choose 'Create Document' to make a new file, then select from one of the many starter templates or just choose 'Blank' if you want to start afresh without help.

Step 2: Putting Pen To Virtual Paper

Writing with Pages is a piece of cake: just touch the page to place the cursor and then type with the virtual keyboard that appears. If you're using a template, you'll see placeholder text, but touch it and start typing and it'll be removed. By default, the Word Count and Check Spelling settings will be on to help you, but you can turn these off by tapping the spanner icon and going into Settings.

iTip – ORGANISE YOUR FILES
Tap and hold on a file on the Documents screen, then drag files together to create folders that can help keep your creations organised into relevant groups.

Step 3: Changing Fonts And Size

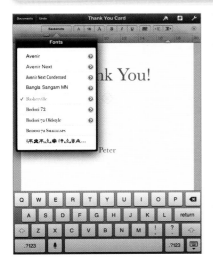

To select any text, double-tap it or triple-tap if you want to select an entire paragraph. Now tap the thin brown line at the top of the screen to reveal the ruler that also contains shortcuts for text styling. You can use these to change the font, increase the size of the text, apply bold, italic or underline styles and alter the alignment, as well as adding hard tabs if you need them.

Step 4: Adding Visual Elements

If you want to add pictures to your document, tap where you'd like it to appear to move the cursor and then touch the plus button on the top bar. From here, you can choose any photo that's in your Camera Roll or Photo Stream, as well as a variety of tables, charts and shapes. You can then move and resize the image by using the blue dots around the outside.

Step 5: Applying Styles

Tap an element on the page, then tap the paintbrush icon on the top bar to apply style changes. The options you get will be context-sensitive depending on what you've selected, such as borders for photos or colours for charts, as well as flipping, scaling and more. Style application also applies to text, as there are a variety of stock text styles like headings or titles.

Step 6: Sharing Your Documents

If you want to get your created files off your iPad, you can tap the spanner icon in the top-right corner and choose 'Share And Print'. If you have an Airprint-compatible printer, then you can print copies off directly from your iPad; if not, you can send the file to iTunes or an iCloud-enabled iDisk, or email it as a Pages file, a PDF or even a Word-compatible document.

iPad mini

How To Use... Numbers

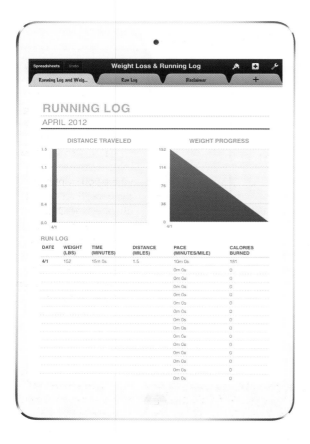

Spreadsheets might be boring, but they're also important. That's why Apple's own version of Excel has made creating and managing them as painless and simple as it can possibly be...

Step 1: Setting Up iCloud

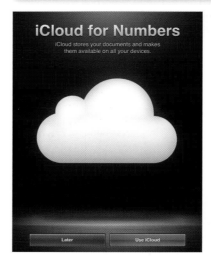

When you first start up Numbers, you'll get the option to activate iCloud and share all the documents you create within it with all your other iOS devices. Obviously, it makes sense to say yes so that everything you do is backed up in case something goes wrong, but you can always go into Settings and find Numbers in the Apps section later if you want to turn it off.

Step 2: Your First Spreadsheet

Select the 'Create A New Spreadsheet' option (or tap 'Spreadsheets' in the top-left corner and then hit '+') and you'll get to choose from all manner of pre-loaded templates. Start with a blank for now. If you want to add another sheet to your document, just tap the manila '+' tab at the top. You can re-order sheets by holding your finger on a tab and then sliding it left or right.

iTip – GET STARTED
Numbers can be as simple or as complex as you like. The 'Getting Started' file on the main spreadsheet page has interactive tutorials that are really useful!

Step 3: Entering Your Info

To add content to your table, double-tap any cell to make the virtual keyboard appear. There are four different keyboards, accessed by the small blue buttons: 42 offers digits, money, percentages and more, Clock lets you put in dates and times, 'T' is for pure text entry like labels and '=' is for formulas that let you add up columns/row, calculate percentages and add complex functions.

Step 4: Creating Charts

Once you have a table full of data, you can automatically convert it into a chart by tapping the plus button in the top-right corner and choosing 'Charts'. Drag the one you want to where you want it on the page, then tap the big blue 'Add Data' button. Tap and drag to select the cells you want featured in your table, then touch the 'Done' button at the top to create the chart.

Step 5: Applying Styles

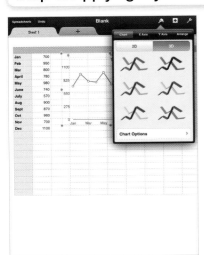

You can also change the style of virtually every element of your spreadsheet by selecting the thing you want to change, then tapping the paintbrush icon in the top-right to bring up a context-sensitive menu. Style changes range from simple things like colour or layout to more in-depth design changes – explore the menus and you'll see just how much there is to alter!

Step 6: Exporting Your Data

Your spreadsheet will automatically be saved in Numbers, so when you open the app again you can access your previous work from the Spreadsheets menu. If you want to be able to use this data in other apps or send it to someone else, though, just tap the Tools menu and you'll see you can send or print your data or save it in a format that can be opened by other programs.

iPad mini

Related Productivity Apps

Let's face it, there's no such thing as being too productive – that's why this range of productivity-assisting apps should go a long way towards making you as busy as a very busy thing indeed!

iTemplates

Price: £1.99 / $2.99
Developed By: Abdullah
In-app Purchases: No

Even though Pages gives you the flexibility to create pretty much any kind of document you like in it with the templates provided, that still requires more effort than some people are willing to give. Enter iTemplates, which has a huge number of pre-built templates for Pages split into 15 different categories – CVs, letters, memos, reports and more. You need Pages to use it, though.

Polaris Office

Price: £16.99 / $19.99
Developed By: Infraware Co. Ltd
In-app Purchases: No

While we still stand by our claim that Apple's range of iWorks apps can provide the perfect word processing, spreadsheet and presentation tools for the iPad, that doesn't mean you're stuck for choice. True, Microsoft doesn't have an Office presence on the App Store, but Polaris Office is pretty much the same thing and even supports documents created in Microsoft format.

Templates For Numbers

Price: £1.99 / $2.99
Developed By: Graphic Node
In-app Purchases: No

Just as iTemplates (covered on the left) adds a wide range of new templates to Apple's Pages app, so Templates For Numbers adds… er, templates for Numbers, obviously. There are 70 new templates available in both A4 and US Letter format that can be edited down into any form you like, and importing them is as simple as choosing the one you want and pressing a button.

TeamViewer

Price: Free
Developed By: TeamViewer
In-app Purchases: No

This app allows secure remote access to any computers or devices connected to it, so if you want to be able to access files on your computer while you're out and about, you can get to all your stuff via your iPad. You can even reboot your computer remotely. The free version is only for personal use, though, and if you're planning to use this in a commercial environment you'd need to shell out £69.99 for the Pro version.

Notability

Price: £1.99 / $1.49
Developed By: Ginger Labs
In-app Purchases: No

Take notes in whatever way suits you best with Notability. The app integrates handwriting, typing, and recording, so you can use whichever method you prefer to keep a record of your thoughts and ideas. You can even use it to annotate PDFs, which are otherwise tricky to edit. Notability can also sync with several cloud services, including Dropbox, to make sure there's always a backup of your work saved somewhere.

SimpleMind+

Price: Free
Developed By: xpt Software & Consulting
In-app Purchases: Yes (full version upgrade)

Have you ever tried mind mapping? It's the process of writing down ideas and then pulling ideas out from those into a giant spiderweb of creativity, which comes in useful when you have a big group of people all thinking about the same thing. SimpleMind+ takes that concept and makes it digital, meaning you can create and then share mind maps at the touch of a button. It's a universal app too, which is nice.

Paper

Price: Free
Developed By: FiftyThree Inc
In-app Purchases: Yes (more tools)

Very little that we can say about Paper will ever be as perfect and 'Wow!' inducing as the video that plays the first time you start the app up. The minute-long clip shows off pretty everything that Paper can do with simple finger strokes, while also proving that it's possibly the most elegant and simple creativity app you'll have ever used. And the best bit? It's totally free. Well, mostly.

At its heart, Paper is a simple sketch app that allows you to draw, write and otherwise put ideas down in solid, shareable form. However, its obviously Japanese stylings combined with a well

conceived design make it so much more than that. The way that it breaks down your productivity into books that are shown on the front page and can be flicked through like any book on the shelf of any book store; the way you can add books or pages to already existing books with just a simple tap, then edit the look and feel of those books and pages with just a few more; the way the brushes actually feel like they're doing what they'd do on real paper and how they react to pressure from your fingertip, even though Paper is a totally digital product... it's really quite astounding when you actually use it.

True, the fact that all bar one of the brushes (Draw) are locked behind in-app purchases might seem like a bit of a con, but it's really not, because you can get all of them in a single bundle for just £5.49, which is a ridiculously cheap price considering the quality of the overall product. In fact, had FiftyThree set Paper's price at double that, we'd probably still pay it. As it is, though, it's free to download and try; trust us though, once you've given it a whirl, you won't disagree with us in the slightest.

Brushes – iPad Edition

Price: £5.49 / $7.99
Developed By: Taptrix Inc
In-app Purchases: No

As far as creative art packages go, they really don't come any more powerful than Brushes. It's an entire paint set in digital form, allowing you to use 19 different brushes and five unique blend modes across up to six different layers (meaning you can edit one part of a painting without having to mess with other bits you're happy with) to create art that's truly awe-inspiring – provided you have the necessary talent to do it, that is. Of course, you don't have to take our word for how much potential Brushes has; if you want actual proof of what can be done with it, all you have to do is sit back and watch this: **www.youtube.com/watch?v=5OLP4nbAVA4**.

MomoNote

Price: £2.99 / $4.99
Developed By: MK HQ
In-app Purchases: No

If you're out and about, there may come a time when you suddenly have a brilliant idea and want to jot it down quickly before you forget it. While the more arty apps like Brushes and Paper can help with that, MomoNote is specifically designed for taking memos and notes that would otherwise get lost on pieces of actual paper. Everything from brilliant ideas to simple reminders and shopping lists can be jotted down instantly, and since this universal app makes use of the cloud, it'll keep all your notes organised across all your iOS devices, meaning you can write something at home on your iPad and then take it with you on your iPhone without having to copy any files over.

Slideshow Remote

Price: £2.99 / $4.99
Developed By: LogicInMind
In-app Purchases: No

What, you're still using PowerPoint to make all your presentations despite us telling you how brilliant Keynote is? Pah, fine. Have it your way. At least know that your iPad can still play a role in the presentation of your, er, presentations thanks to this handy little app. Not only does it act as a viewer for both PowerPoint and Keynote documents received via email, but you can also link up your iPad to act as a Wi-Fi-enabled remote for a laptop running PowerPoint presentations. It comes with a variety of mouse settings and while it can take a little bit of fiddling to set up (since you need specific software to get it going), the results are definitely worth it.

Your iPad mini And...
Education

It comes as little surprise that more and more schools and colleges are investing in iPads and iPad minis as learning aids, given just what an abundance of educational possibilities the devices have managed to open up.

Not for the first time, we suspect it comes down to a touch-screen interface. For very young children, not having to learn the ins and outs of a keyboard and mouse means that they can get right down to business, intuitively working with some of the many high-quality apps that are available to help them with their learning. Granted, younger users tend to leave mucky fingerprints all over the screen, but they're easily cleaned up afterwards. Furthermore, they offer ample evidence as to just how robust the iPad mini actually is (even though we wouldn't recommend putting that to the test if you can help it!)

It's not just a device for the very young, though, as the iPad mini opens up educational possibilities for those of all ages looking to learn. Some of which we're going to be concentrating on in this very chapter.

In particular, we're going to take a closer look at iTunes U from Apple in the pages that lie ahead. iTunes U brings together a brilliant collection of courses and resources all in one place. It sounds clichéd, but there's really a lot of substance to it: this is a classroom in your hands, and you can choose to subscribe to whatever courses happen to interest you. There's an almost-bewildering selection for you to choose from!

If you're looking to explore things fully off your own back, though, then there's the wealth of electronic books just waiting to be discovered. Even the iPad mini with the smallest capacity – currently sitting at 16GB – can hold a huge number of books, and if you're embarking on a big research project, for instance, this might be just the ticket.

Finally, the App Store is a haven for a large collection of high-quality educational downloads, again targeting a broad collection of subjects and age ranges. We have some recommendations for you to set you on your way....

How To Use... iTunes U

Your iPad isn't just for keeping you entertained: it can also be used as a study tool. iTunes U makes a whole library of texts, videos and lectures available to you at the touch of a button

Step 1: Downloading iTunes U

Although the name suggests that iTunes U should come pre-loaded on your iPad, it's actually available for download from the App Store. The good news is that it's free, so you won't have to pay for it; the better news is that it's a universal app, so if you have an iPhone or iPod Touch as well as an iPad, you can take your learning with you wherever you go.

Step 2: Syncing Your Course Information

When you first start up iTunes U, you'll be asked to allow it to send you push notifications (which is handy for when new coursework becomes available) and to sync your notes/course information. Syncing makes all of your study materials available on all of your iOS devices, so it's quite important if you plan to use multiple devices. You can always turn it on or off via the Settings menu later, if you change your mind.

iTip – FREE SAMPLE
iTunes U lets you try out all kinds of courses, so if there's anything you've ever fancied studying, now's your chance to get a free taster...

Step 3: The Course Library

The first screen might look familiar if you've used iBooks or Newsstand; it's a storage library that shows all the courses that you've downloaded using the app. Initially, it'll be empty, unless you have previously stored work on another iOS device, in which case it'll sync the information in the account to match. To start filling it up, you'll need to pay a visit to the iTunesU catalogue.

Step 4: The iTunes U Catalog

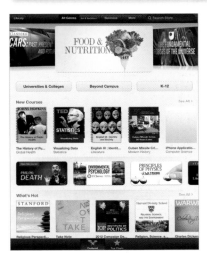

Not surprisingly, the iTunes U catalogue, which you can access by pressing the 'Catalog' button in the top-left corner of the library screen, is much like the App and iTunes stores. The main screen shows you new courses and those that are proving popular, as well as a selection of promoted topics, but you can also search depending on what you're interested in.

Step 5: Pick Your Learning Level

The catalogue is split into three levels of learning: 'Universities & Colleges', 'Beyond Campus' and 'K-12'. The first speaks for itself, while the second is aimed at wider learning from places like art institutes and academies. K-12 refers to lower-level learning ranging from nursery to college students. Each offers a wide range of institutions for you to learn from.

Step 6: Browsing Institutions

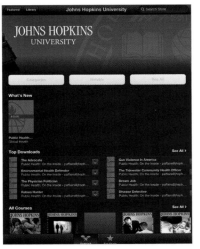

To check out the different institutions available on iTunes U, just tap one of the three buttons on the front page to bring up a scrollable menu. The majority of institutions are US-based (including famous ones like Yale and Harvard), although there are others from around the world in there too. Tap a name to see all the courses available from that institution.

iPad mini

How To Use… iTunes U (continued)

Step 7: Searching For Specifics

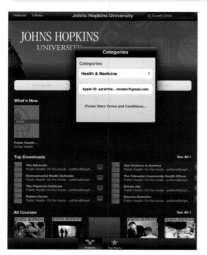

You can search for courses in two ways: either use the 'Categories' button on any institution to browse through subjects or tap the 'Search' tab in the top-right and type something in. This will bring up a list of courses that match your search. Keep it as simple as possible, though, because being too specific will obviously give you fewer results to look through.

Step 8: Checking Course Details

To read more about a particular course, simply type it and you'll get a detailed information screen giving more background, a course outline showing all the modules and any reviews it has been given by other iTunes U users. You can also tap on the 'Materials' button to see what kind of things are available for download such as documentation, coursework or video tutorials, for example.

Step 9: Subscribing To A Course

When you've found a course that you want to download, hit the grey 'Subscribe Free' button and then 'Get Course' when it turns green. This then adds the course list to your library shelf, but it doesn't download any of the content for that course; you do that yourself from within the course content. Return to the library by tapping the 'Library' button in the top-left of the store.

Step 10: Beginning Your Course

Tap the course book on your library shelf to open it and you can get learning! You'll see four tabs down the side: 'Info' gives you details of your course (tap the 'Info' button at the top to see more), 'Posts' gives you a list of lessons available, 'Notes' is where you can write your own notes (obviously!) and 'Materials' enables you to download the various materials needed for the course.

Step 11: The Posts Tab

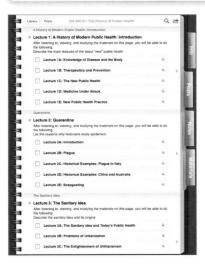

Not surprisingly, you'll spend most of your time on the 'Posts' tab, as it's here that you can access each stage of your chosen course. Tap the arrow on the right of a lesson to see a full explanation, as well as a list of the materials necessary. You can tap the small checkbox next to each material to keep tabs on which ones you've already read, viewed or otherwise used.

Step 12: Downloading Materials

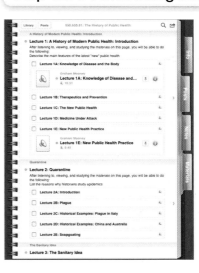

Although you can download materials in the 'Materials' tab, it's best done from within the lesson descriptions on the 'Posts' tab so you know which you currently need. Tap a material to expand it; you can tap the 'Info' button to get more information or the arrow button to download it directly to your iPad. Make sure you have enough storage space for video tutorials!

Step 13: Viewing Materials

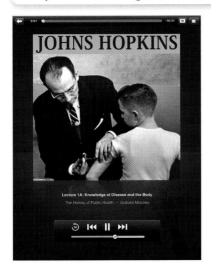

Once your materials have downloaded (which might take a while if it's a video tutorial, as they're usually quite big), you can view them by tapping the relevant section. Documents and transcripts open in iBooks, PDFs open within iTunes U itself and video tutorials open with the Video app. You can also view them outside of iTunes U using these apps from the home screen.

Step 14: Adding Notes

Chances are you'll want to take notes of your own throughout the duration of your course. While you can do that with good old pen and paper, iTunes U also lets you do it digitally. Just tap the Notes tab inside any course book and then press the plus button in the top-right corner and type away on the virtual keyboard. It also supports Dictation, so you can think out loud!

iPad mini

How To Use... iBooks

Apple's iBooks app turns your iPad into a library packed with everything you could ever want to read. Why bother carrying bulky printed titles around with you when you can fit hundreds in your pocket at once?

Step 1: Adding New Books To Your Library

Once you download iBooks for free from the App Store, open it and tap Store in the top-left. From here you can browse or search for books, both free and paid for. Tap the grey box displaying the price, then tap it again when it turns green and enter your Apple ID. You could also tap 'Get Sample' if you aren't quite sure whether you want to purchase a book yet.

Step 2: Adding PDFs To iBooks

You can also add PDFs (a form of digital document) to iBooks. If you find a PDF online, view it through your iPad and tap it to get an 'Open In iBooks' option. If you've been emailed a PDF, just open the attachment and tap 'Open In iBooks'. Once you have some, there'll be an option to switch between books and PDFs near the top of the library screen.

Step 3: Browsing Your Library

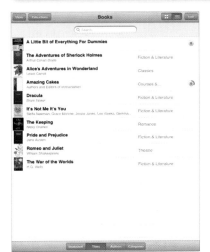

Once your library starts to fill up, you need an easy way to find stuff, and while the bookshelf looks nice, it's not easy to tell what's what. If you swipe down the screen you can change to list view using the icon with three horizontal lines. Then you just simply browse via title, author or category. You can also use the search function near the top of the screen.

Step 4: Syncing/Adding Bookmarks

If you have multiple Apple devices, you can use synced bookmarks to start reading on one and continue on another. Go into Settings, tap iBooks on the left and turn on 'Sync Bookmarks'. You can add bookmarks by tapping a page and then the symbol in the top-right corner. To see your bookmarks, tap the symbol on the left with the three dots and lines.

Step 5: Formatting Book Text

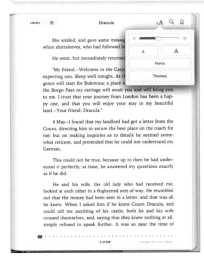

To change how the text in a book looks, tap on a page and then the symbol at the top with a small and large 'A'. On the overlay, you can alter the text size (tap the smaller or larger 'A') to make it more visible, change the font used for displaying the text and even view your books in an attractive sepia tone, which is easier for some to read than the harsher black on white.

Step 6: Use The Dictionary

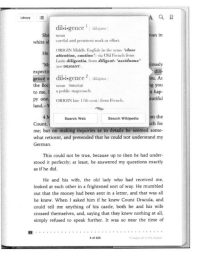

If you ever find yourself wondering what a word means, you can tap and hold your finger on any word in any book to have four different options pop up. Tapping 'Dictionary' from this selection will provide an in-depth definition of the highlighted word, along with examples of how it can be used in everyday language, its origin and any derivatives in a nicely presented form.

iPad mini

Related Education Apps

The best e-readers and the finest in poetry, intellectual discussion, children's teaching and much, much more. Whatever your learning-related poison, there's a huge range of apps to suit your educational ambitions…

Reading Trainer

Price: £2.99 / $4.99
Developed By: HeKu IT
In-app Purchases: No

Taking the opportunity to read more? Well, good for you. That said, though, you may need to brush up on your skills if it's been a while, which is where this app comes in handy. Reading Trainer is a highly acclaimed, award-winning app that can greatly increase your reading speed and mental capacity with a variety of exercises, plus a plan that charts your progress. It works too!

Dictionary.com

Price: Free
Developed By: Dictionary.com, LLC
In-app Purchases: No

Really, this is something that everyone should have use for, but it's especially useful for students. This dictionary app contains definitions for a million words, plus 90,000 synonyms and antonyms in the thesaurus (and let's face it, if you just had to look up 'antonym' to find out what we meant, this is definitely for you). Best of all, it doesn't require an Internet connection to work.

TED

Price: Free
Developed By: TED Conferences
In-app Purchases: No

They're not quite learning lectures, but TED's extensive series of talks given by highly influential and fascinating people are definitely worth checking out if you want to be inspired. There are over 1,100 videos available that can be streamed directly to your iPad, downloaded for watching later or even sent over Airplay to your TV for big-screen viewing. It also includes audio lectures.

Waterstones For iPad

Price: Free
Developed By: Waterstones
In-app Purchases: Yes (printed books)

If you're a proper student at a real educational institution and have a desperate need for printed studying material, Waterstones (yes, the book store) has the app for you. Use it to browse and buy a huge range of books for delivery to your home, check stock in your local stores in case you want to go and pick it up yourself and even write reviews for your books when you're done with them. Who said print is dead?

Stanza

Price: Free
Developed By: Lexcycle
In-app Purchases: No

Stanza is a free ebook reader that's a pretty good alternative to iBooks. There are over 50,000 books available to buy and read on this platform, and another 50,000 free classics available from Project Gutenberg and its ilk. Comics and graphic novels can also be downloaded and read through Stanza. On the iPad, your reading material will look particularly clean and crisp, which makes for a pleasant reading experience.

Maths Age 3-5

Price: Free
Developed By: Eurotalk
In-app Purchases: Yes (additional topics)

Giving your kids a leg-up on learning is always a good idea before they head to school, so this pre-school app comes in handy for getting them ahead in maths. The free version comes with the first topic (sorting and matching) for free and then if your child thinks it's great, you can purchase the other nine topics either individually for 69p or as a bundle for £5. It even has an interactive 'teacher' to help get the basics across.

Google Play Books

Price: Free
Developed By: Google
In-app Purchases: Yes (ebooks)

Ten years ago, Google was little more than the software that Yahoo! used for internet searches; now it's one of the biggest and most important tech companies in the world, as well as a verb used in daily speech by pretty much everyone. That's why it should come as no surprise to anyone that Google has decided to enter the competitive e-reader arena with Play Books, it's own take on the services already offered by Amazon and Apple.

Much like its competitors, Google Play Books offers access to more than three million books, free preview pages to try out before you commit to a purchase, a night-reading mode and some control over the fonts and line spacing of the text. Best of all, though, it syncs effortlessly across devices so if you're reading on your iPhone on the bus, you can continue from where you left off reading on your iPad at home.

To its credit, Google Play Books has the most simplistic interface of the major e-readers and, in some ways, is the nicest to use thanks to its accessibility. However, while it's a perfectly good e-reader app, the fact is that it isn't quite as polished as either iBooks or Kindle, so the appeal for an iPad owner might be a little bit limited when you can use one of the other services instead. Nevertheless, the book pricing seems to be ever so slightly lower than its competitors and it's a free app, so by all means give it a whirl - it can only improve, after all.

Poetry from The Poetry Foundation

Price: Free
Developed By: The Poetry Foundation
In-app Purchases: No

If you're a student studying the art of prose or even just a fan of poetry in all its forms, then this great free app gives you the opportunity to take a break from the hustle of everyday life and enjoy some quality wordsmithery. Although there are some notable exceptions from the list available (what, no Larkin?), there's still a huge range of greats to choose from ranging from Eliot and Dickinson and The Bard himself. Not sure what to read? Simply give your iPad a shake to discover a new poem! You can also search for a poem when you only know a single line of it, as well as easily share your favourite poems over various social networking site likes Facebook.

The Elementals

Price: Free
Developed By: Angry Robot Zombie Factory
In-app Purchases: No

So you want to try to learn all the elements of the periodic table but don't really know where to start. Surely there has to be an app for that, right? Not surprisingly, there is and, even better, it's one that isn't boring. Okay, so maybe what The Angry Robot Zombie Factory has done isn't exactly revolutionary: it's taken each element of the table and not only colour-coded them, but then given them a bit of personality by adding eyes and the ability to flick them around the screen a bit. Still, it's still more fun than staring at a piece of paper for hours on end, hoping that the information will burrow its way into your brain and since it's free, you don't have to buy a chart.

Kindle

Price: Free
Developed By: AMZN Mobile LLC
In-app Purchases: Yes (ebooks)

You're probably aware that the Kindle is Amazon's own e-reader device and comes in various different forms. Not surprisingly, the Kindle App does its best to replicate that experience on your iPad, rivalling Apple's own iBooks service. There are over 900,000 books to choose from (with more every week!) and plenty of free samples, while the text can be customised to suit. A handy email address allows you to send PDFs and other documents to your Kindle app and due to the beautifully named Whispersync technology, your reading remains uninterrupted: if you go from reading on your iPad Kindle app to your Kindle device, it'll remember exactly where you left off. Lovely.

iPad mini

Related Education Apps (continued)

Molecules

Price: Free
Developed By: Sunset Lake Software
In-app Purchases: No

Science students, rejoice: thanks to Molecules, you'll never have to play with plastic balls and rods again to prove that your theory of quantum physics is right! Well, maybe. In any case, Molecules lets you render and view 3D representations of molecules (as the name suggests) and then play with them to your heart's content. It also has a direct link to the Protein Data Bank (that's good, right?).

SpeedReader

Price: £1.49 / $1.99
Developed By: ComputerDocs LLC
In-app Purchases: No

Burn through books at speed with the help of this speed-focused reading app. It comes loaded with a selection of classic books, and you just decide how fast you reckon you can go and set it running. Depending on your settings, you'll see the book flash by as either a sequence of words or phrases. It's not for anyone who wants to savour literature, but for grabbing a quick overview.

iGeology

Price: Free
Developed By: British Geological Survey
In-app Purchases: No

No, you can't use it to find dinosaurs or plan out a journey to the centre of the earth. However, what you can do is use iGeology to explore the geology of your local area or, indeed, anywhere in the UK. Simply type in the name of a location or a postcode, and the app will use the British Geological Survey's national scale maps to show you exactly what kind of things lie beneath your feet.

StudyAtOU

Price: Free
Developed By: The Open University
In-app Purchases: No

While The Open University has a presence on iTunes U, the real OU is the only place where you can get proper qualifications that are recognised by employers the world over. If taking such a course interests you, then this app might come in handy. Sure, it's little more than an interactive prospectus and would have been better if you could use it to actually do the courses, but it's still useful to see what's available.

Audiobooks

Price: Free
Developed By: Cross Forward Consulting
In-app Purchases: Yes (books)

If you'd rather listen to your books than read them, this is the app for you. There are thousands of free audiobooks available for download, all professionally narrated so you get to hear the writing at its best. You can skip, pause, and navigate each book by chapter, and the iTunes-esque app is simple to navigate and easy to control. More free books are being added all the time, while newer books are being made available as paid downloads.

Shakespeare

Price: Free
Developed By: Readdle
In-app Purchases: No

We'll give you three guesses what this app's all about. Give up? It's the Bard, obviously, and all his work therein. This app features the complete works of Shakespeare (41 plays, 154 sonnets and six poems) and comes with features such as detailed scene breakdowns, a random quote generator and a Shakespeare Passport that gives you exclusive benefits when you show it at Shakespeare-related events.

Star Walk For iPad

Price: £2.99 / $4.99
Developed By: Vito Technology Inc.
In-app Purchases: No

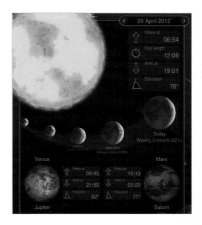

Although it certainly helps to have a passing interest, the truth is that you don't have to be into astronomy to get enjoyment out of the stars. Heck, you don't even need to have a telescope or any books about the subject to dip your toe in the space waters. All you need is Star Walk for your iPad and you're ready to go.

Designed specifically for the iPad 2 and later iPads (so you iPad mini will be fine), Star Walk provides on-the-spot information about the stars in the sky depending on where you are in the world. Just hold your iPad up in front of you and the app will use augmented reality and GPS technology to map out the sky as it is right at that precise second, allowing you to see exactly what you're looking at. On top of that, you can instantly see where constellations and planets are just by tapping the search list and choosing a name or zoom in on any specific star, galaxy or planet and tap the 'i' button to get more data about it.

Star Walk also has the ability to actively track the International Space Station, display star/planet positions for any time or date that you tell it and display in Night Mode so that you don't lose sight of the stars. It also has a library of astronomical photos that are updated daily with truly amazing photos taken of both the stars and the earth, which can then be downloaded to your Camera Roll or shared with friends via Facebook or Twitter should you wish.

Autism Apps

Price: Free
Developed By: Touch Autism
In-app Purchases: No

If you're one of the many people with children suffering from learning disabilities, it can sometimes be hard to know where to turn when it comes to helping them learn. Thankfully, this app has be designed specifically to pull together details about every app that can assist with special needs learning and covers a variety of disabilities including autism and Down syndrome. Each listing includes as much information as possible about the app so that you can see if it's suitable for your needs, while the list is split into over 30 different categories to make it easier to find the right app. You can also sort apps depending on whether they're free or cost money.

The Cat In The Hat

Price: £2.49 / $2.99
Developed By: Oceanhouse Media
In-app Purchases: No

Dr Seuss's *The Cat in the Hat* has helped generations of kids learn how to read, and there's no reason it should stop now. This app turns the classic book into an interactive storytelling experience: there are three reading modes, with professional narration and fun sound effects, and every page features objects you can tap to get more info or pronunciation guides. Parents and children can even record their own voices, and share their own versions of the story with other users of the app. The artwork is familiar, nostalgic, and just as quirky as ever. Children will barely even notice they're supposed to be being educated while they're watching the exploits of that naughtiest of cats...

Literary Analysis Guide

Price: £1.99 / $2.99
Developed By: Gatsby's Light
In-app Purchases: No

Are you not quite sure how syntax differs from grammar but always wanted to find out? Then you'd better get this app. Literary Analysis Guide is perfect for anyone studying literature at a higher level or anyone who just likes delving into its inner workings for fun (although we're not sure who that is). An innovative wheel-based interface allows you to quickly find out more about the component literary devices involved with poetry, prose and rhetoric, and how these devices are employed within the literature you're studying. Developed by an English professor, Literary Analysis guide is perfect for anyone from teenagers up to other English professors.

Your iPad mini And…
Photography & Video

Built into the iPad mini, as you may already have noticed, is a capable camera, which is able to capture good-quality still photos, and high-definition video. Thus, it's not just a device for watching other people's video and photographic work; the iPad mini also has the tools at hand to let you make your own.

We're going to start in this chapter with the basics. We're going to take you through the built-in camera and how to work your way around the provided camera app. We'll address issues such as lighting and composition and then take you through how to manage the material that you capture to your iPad mini.

Furthermore, we'll then go into a little more detail on what you can do with your pictures and video. Thus, we're going to take a look at iPhoto and tools that it offers to allow you to touch

up, crop, adjust and mess around with your photos. We'll go through everything from applying special effects through to sharing the end product.

On the video side, the iMovie app puts a lot of power at your fingertips. You can edit your videos, add captions, insert the music of your choice, rearrange clips and a whole lot more. Again, we're going to take you through all of that, as well as how to share your work at the end of it all.

Finally, we're exploring the App Store again and the many alternative tools that are available to download. There's an amazing amount your iPad mini can do when it comes to your photos and video, and you might just be surprised at how intuitive it all is.

iPad mini

How To Use... Camera

It's all very well knowing how to use a camera – you point, you click, that's it – but to get the most out of the Camera app that comes pre-loaded with your iPad mini, you'll need a few pointers…

Step 1: Off To A Quick Start

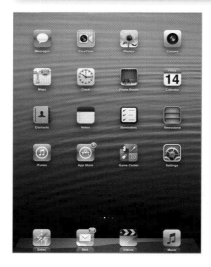

The Camera app comes pre-loaded on your iPad, so to launch it, just tap the icon on your home screen. Your iPad has two cameras - one in the front and one in the back - which makes it handy for taking self-portraits as well as using it as a more traditional camera. There aren't many options built into the default Camera app, though, which we go into in more detail elsewhere in this book.

Step 2: Check The Lighting

Unlike the iPhone, your iPad mini doesn't have a built-in flash, which means you'll need to be aware of the lighting when you're taking a photo. In lower light, you're likely to get grainy images or even pictures that just don't come out at all, so try to take pictures in natural light if at all possible or at least in a place where you can make sure there's enough light to get a decent snap.

iTip – USING DIGITAL ZOOM
Zooming in and out is as easy as using the pinch/stretch movement with your fingers. Just touch the screen and pinch them together or stretch them apart to do it.

Step 3: Composing A Shot

Selecting the 'Options' button at the top of the screen enables you to turn on a grid, which overlays lines onto your viewfinder. You can use this to help with the composing of your shots, either by making sure your subject is framed nicely in the middle of the shot (no cut-off heads here!) or by using photography's 'rule of three' to get the balance right in your pictures.

Step 4: Changing Your Focus

The iPad has a pretty decent auto-focus feature, but it'll usually focus on the image in the middle of the screen. If you'd actually prefer to focus on something else, then it's possible to refocus the camera to whatever part of the picture you want to concentrate your shot on. Simply touch the object you want to focus on and the camera will do the rest for you!

Step 5: Take And Check Your Photos

Once your shot is properly set up, just touch the camera icon to take the picture. Once you've taken a photo, the Camera app will automatically get ready to take another one, but if you want to check how your last picture turned out, you can just swipe to the right to pull it up on the screen. If you're happy, great! If you're not, just take another one; after all, it's not like you're wasting film.

Step 6: Photo Storage

All the photos you've taken on your iPad will be stored in the Camera Roll section of the Photos App, which you'll also find sitting on your home screen. You can easily organise, share, edit or delete them from here. Due to its size, the iPad isn't an ideal camera, which might be why there are so few features in this app, but if you really need to snap a picture and it's all you have, then it'll do.

iPad mini

How To Use... Photos

There are a number of handy tools built into the Photos app on your iPad that can help you to manage and organise your photographs, so it's worth familiarising yourself with them so you're not left struggling to find your pictures…

Step 1: Setting Up iCloud

Although your iPad stores your photos safely in the Camera Roll, it's best to have a backup of everything in case something goes wrong. You can do this through iCloud: go to 'Settings' > 'iCloud' > 'Photo Stream' and turn it on to keep all your photos safely stored in the cloud. You can also back up your photos to your computer using the data cable that came with your iPad, to be doubly safe!

Step 2: Creating A New Album

All your photos are stored in the 'Photos' tab of the Photos App, but to tidy things up a bit and make your photos easier to find, you might want to sort them into albums. Touch the 'Albums' tab and you'll see just one album: Camera Roll. Touch the plus icon in the top left of the screen to make a new album, and give it a meaningful title.

Step 3: Filling Your New Album

Once you type in a name for your album, you can select images from your iPad to add to it. Any you pick will then appear in the new album, but won't be deleted from any other albums they're in; they'll still be in Camera Roll and Photo Stream, for instance. Deleting them from these two places will delete them permanently, so be careful before choosing to do so.

Step 4: Sharing An Image

To send a photograph to someone else, view the image on-screen and then click on the arrow icon in the top right. You'll now have a number of options, including emailing your message, sending it as a message, printing it out, using it as wallpaper or even assigning it to a contact, which means you'll see their photo whenever they call or message you.

Step 5: Publishing Photos To Twitter

To share your images wider than just an email or a text, you can also send it to Twitter straight from Photos. Selecting the 'Twitter' option will enable you to enter a short message to accompany your picture, then automatically add a Twitpic link to your image. Of course, you need to have a Twitter account set up on your iPad mini beforehand for this to work.

Step 6: Other Photo Options

Using Air Print, you can print your images provided you have a compatible printer associated with your iPad. In addition, you can set any photograph as your wallpaper (see elsewhere in this book for full details of how to do that), or assign it to a contact, meaning that particular image will be displayed every time that person contacts you.

iPhoto

Price: £2.99 / $4.99
Developed By: Apple
In-App Purchases: No

Previously the only element of iLife lacking an app version, iPhoto eventually joined the ranks of iMovie and Garageband to let you edit, manage and display your photos from the comfort of your iPad mini…

It always seemed somewhat odd to us that while every other component of the iLife suite (a package of lifestyle software created by Apple for its Mac computers) had its own app-based equivalent, iPhoto was mysteriously absent. For those who loved to use their iPads or iPhones to capture video and then edit it together for portable playback, there was a cut-down version of iMovie; for the budding musician on the go who wanted to always have a means of capturing inspiration wherever they were, the Garageband app was always there. But the photography buffs who wanted to keep their snapshot memories perfectly organised and tweaked with all kinds of lighting, colour and specialist filters? They had to get their kicks from the likes of Photoshop Express and other, less impressive knockoff imitations.

Or, at least, they did until Apple got its house in order and finally bothered releasing an iOS version of iPhoto. We'd be annoyed that it's taken so long to get around to it, but… well, it's hard to be cross when the result is a photography manipulation app that blows away everything else available right now. Okay, so maybe it's not the be-all and end-all of photo fiddling (for truly expert editing, you're still best off using proper software on

Above: iPhoto has a lot of sophisticated options, but most of them are ridiculously easy to work with

a computer like Adobe Photoshop), but when you're essentially paying £3 for what is essentially a hefty beast of a creativity app, what's here is still enough to keep even semi-professional people happy for a very long time.

Not surprisingly, it's the ease of use combined with some pretty in-depth tools that makes iPhoto on iOS something special. Each of the included tools does something pretty obvious – cropping and rotating, adjusting brightness, contrast and colour, applying effects with brushes and filters – and they offer enough levels of control to be used to great or subtle effect. However, each also works with a single touch (or, in some cases, multi-finger touches) and it only takes a simple drag of a finger to make small or drastic changes to any photograph you import into iPhoto.

It has plenty of other neat little touches too, such as the ability to edit the angle of your photos using the iPad's gyroscope rather than your fingers, touching and holding down two fingers to bring up a magnifying lens that can then be twisted as you would a real-world lens to zoom in further, or automatically compiling selected photos into a ready-made montage of memories to show your friends. Sure, they're all a bit gimmicky, but it's little things like these that really set Apple's product apart from the rest of the crowd.

And as you might expect, iPhoto's connectivity not just with the 'big' version of the software but also with a whole host of other social media sources (Facebook, Flickr, iTunes, the iPad's built-in email and more besides) that can be accessed at the touch of a virtual button makes it the perfect way to share your images with the world. Much like every other Apple app take on its various software packages, iPhoto's size and price acts as a cover for what's actually an incredibly advanced, yet totally accessible bit of kit. Why it took them so long to release it alongside the other iLife apps, we're not sure; we're just glad that it got there eventually.

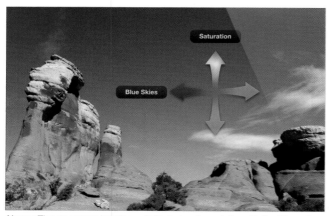

Above: The on-screen interface of iPhoto has been fully optimised to make use of touch screen interaction

How To Use... iPhoto

Considering that it's so cheap, it's really rather amazing how many different tools and editing options have been crammed into iPhoto. And even better, it's so ridiculously easy to use!

Step 1: Importing Photos Into iPhoto

There's no option to take photos directly in iPhoto, but you can immediately access all the pictures in your Camera Roll and iCloud Photo Stream when you start the app. You can also import photos into iPhoto by using iTunes on a computer, wirelessly 'beaming' them from an iOS device running iPhoto or importing them from a camera (although this requires a special connection kit).

Step 2: Using The Thumbnail Grid

Once you select an album source for your image, you'll move to a viewing area where you can see your pictures in full. Swipe left/right on the thumbnail grid at the bottom to scroll through your images and touch one to display it. You can also see info about the photo by tapping the 'i' button in the top-right and hide the grid by tapping the small grid button, top-left.

iPad mini

125

How To Use... iPhoto (continued)

Step 3: Entering Edit mode

Now you've selected a picture, you can get on with editing it to your liking. Tap the 'Edit' button in the top-right corner of the screen and a new bar of icons will appear across the bottom. These are your editing tools. You can start using any of them just by tapping the one you want; once you've made adjustments, tapping the tool again closes it down and stores your changes.

Step 4: Undoing/Redoing Actions

Before you start playing around with your photos, make a note of the most important button of all: undo. It's the curved arrow on the left-hand side of the top bar (*not* the one in the box on the right!). Tap it to undo the last action you performed or hold your finger on it to get the option to undo or redo an action. Handy if you make a mistake while editing photos!

Step 5: Cropping, Scaling And Straightening

The first edit tool on the bottom bar is the crop tool, but it can do more than just slice into images. Using the central box as a guide, you can use one finger to find the part of your picture you want to crop around and two fingers to zoom in/out. You can also use the dial at the bottom to rotate the picture; tapping it lets you do this by tilting the iPad left or right.

Step 6: Brightness And Contrast

The next icon, the small shutter, is for brightness And contrast adjustments. You can drag the outer markers at the bottom (black for shadow, white for highlights) inwards to lighten/darken them, while the same goes for the contrast and sun icons. Alternatively, hold your finger on the photo to activate context-sensitive controls based on what you're touching.

iTip – RESTORE THE ORIGINAL
You can revert to the original version of your photo by touching the curled paper icon next to the 'Edit' button. This will always be preserved, so you can't save over it.

Step 7: Colour Adjustments

The palette icon activates the colour adjustment tools. These are split into 'Colour Saturation', 'Blue Skies', 'Greenery and Skin Tones' and can again be slid left/right to alter the relevant part of your photo. Touching/holding on the photo once again activates context-sensitive controls, while there are also white balance options under the WB icon in the bottom-right corner.

Step 8: Brush-based Editing

Touch the brush icon and you'll see there are a whole host of brushes you can use to touch up your photos: lighten/darken, sharpen/soften, saturate/desaturate and even one for red-eye. These effects are subtle and require direct application to the photo with a finger: use two fingers to zoom in/out and move the photo around while applying these different effects.

Step 9: Special Effects

The final option – the star icon – is for adding effects. There are six categories with all kind of filter styles including vintage photos, colour palettes and even changing your picture into a watercolour painting. Touch the different images at the bottom to change filter or touch the hinge on the right to access the main effect library if you want to change category.

Step 10: Sharing Your Photos

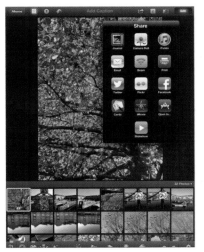

Not surprisingly, iPhoto has plenty of sharing options hidden under the boxed arrow icon including Facebook, Twitter, Flickr, email and more. You can also save it to your Camera Roll here. Best of all, though, is the Journal option: you can add a selection of images at once and iPhoto will compile them into a tasteful montage that will keep the memories of the moment alive.

iPad mini

How To Use... Camera As A Video Recorder

It's not just stills photography that the iPad mini can do. There's also a fully functioning video recorder packed in there as well that can record hours of moving footage - perfect for capturing those spur-of-the-moment events!

Step 1: Accessing The Video Recorder

Unlike most of the other features of your iPad, which all have their own individual apps, the video recorder functions aren't stand-alone. Instead, they're hidden inside the Camera app. If you open Camera and look in the lower-left corner of the screen, there's a little flick switch with two icons: a stills camera and a video camera. Flick this switch to the right to access video mode.

Step 2: Using The Video Recorder

Not surprisingly, taking videos using the Camera app is simple: you just point your iPad at whatever you want to record and press the big red record button at the bottom. It'll keep recording until you press the button again, but be aware that video footage can take up a lot of storage space; if your iPad is full of other content, you might not have much room.

iTip – OVERWRITING VIDEOS

If you pick 'Trim Original' when editing your video down, the full-length version will be deleted forever. Don't do it unless you're absolutely sure you don't need it!

Step 3: Video Recording Options

Unfortunately, there aren't very many options to use while recording video with your iPad. You can turn the flash on or off to help brighten up the scene, touch the screen to choose a focal point or switch from the rear to front-side camera, but the zoom functions of the photo camera aren't available. If you want to zoom in on something, you need to move closer to it!

Step 4: Accessing Your Videos

When you've recorded a video, you'll find it waiting for you in your photo library. Just swipe your finger to the right across the screen while using the Camera app or press the small image in the lower-right corner to access it. Tap the arrow to play the video, then tap the screen again to bring up controls for pausing, deleting or sharing your video with your friends.

Step 5: Skipping And Sharing Videos

The bar at the top of the video is the timeline. You can touch this anywhere and drag your finger left or right to skip through the video to the bit you want. If you touch the arrow button at the bottom, you can also email or send the video via text message to your friends, or even upload it directly to YouTube if you have an account set up and use the YouTube app to log into it.

Step 6: Trimming Your Videos

If you want to trim your video down to only show the important part, touch the left edge of the timeline until it's highlighted and drag it inwards to where you want the video to start, then repeat with the right edge for where it should end. Tap 'Trim' and then select either 'Save To New File' to create a new edited version or 'Trim Original' to save over the old version.

iPad mini

iMovie

Price: £2.99 / $4.99
Developed By: Apple
In-app Purchases: No

So you've recorded some video but think it needs some fine-tuning before you share it? You don't need a computer or fancy software: the iPad mini version of iMovie can do it all for you!

There was a time when editing video captured on a camcorder was laborious and expensive. You needed the right camera kit, obviously, but then there was the technology needed to transfer that footage into an editable format, not to mention the skills to use it. To say it was fiddly is an understatement, especially since everything had to be done in real-time.

Of course, computers changed all that in terms of the kit needed and the fact that you could edit chunks of footage without the need to spool through it, but it didn't make it any less expensive. Even today, it can be costly. Apple's own Final Cut Pro X, possibly the most advanced video editing software available today, comes in at a whopping £200 and with good reason: it's used by professional video editors around the world and has all the tools required to create videos of unequalled standards. Thankfully, though, that doesn't mean high-quality video editing is beyond the reach of the average person, and thanks to Apple packing many of the same tools from Final Cut into another more accessible piece of software, pretty much anyone can make videos that they'd be proud to show off.

Amazingly, you can pick up the Mac version of iMovie – Apple's slimmed down but still impressive video editing software – as part of the iLife package for a mere £40. Even more amazingly, though, you can get the iPad version for the same price as a McDonalds breakfast, with the added bonus that it's far more satisfying when you're done with it. And best of all, the iPad app contains a large number of the functions of its big brother, at not only a fraction of the price but also in an entirely portable form that means you can record video and then immediately edit it down with effects and other tweaks before sharing it in a variety of ways.

Despite being far more advanced than you'd expect a super-cheap mobile video-editing suite to be, the iPad version of iMovie is ridiculously easy to use thanks to its intuitive interface and simple 'drag and drop' controls. Thanks to its integration with the iPad's other apps like Camera and Photos, importing videos into it is a doddle: you just tap, select and you're away. There's also the option to record videos straight into iMovie, then edit them immediately without even having to leave the app.

Above: It seems unlikely, but iMovie on the iPad is insanely close in competency to its bigger computer-based cousin.

And if you have videos on your computer, you can also import those into iMovie by hooking your iPad up to iTunes (although they need to be in the right format for iMovie to understand).

You can even share projects across multiple devices (iPhone, iPod Touch, iPad and Mac computer) through iTunes, meaning you can start editing on the iPhone when you're out and about, then transfer to the iPad or your Mac when you get home. And since the app itself is a universal one across all of Apple's portable devices, you won't have to pay again to keep the project going elsewhere – just re-download the app and pick up where you left off.

Admittedly, you can't expect the kind of toolset that the big version of iMovie offers, but if we're honest, the smaller version isn't all that far off. Aside from a few more captioning options and all the intro/outro stuff that comes with all the additional themes, it's relatively identical. And considering both the price and the portability of the app (just £3!), what's offered by iMovie for iPad is more than enough to justify its usefulness. It won't make you the next Martin Scorsese, but everyone's got to start somewhere and once you've edited your first few videos using the iPad, you might just get a taste for it and take things even further…

How To Use... iMovie

Don't be fooled by the small size and even small price. The iPad version of iMovie is perfect for editing down your videos and turning them into something you'll be proud to show off!

Step 1: The Project Screen

When you first open iMovie, the only thing you'll be able to do is tap the plus button at the bottom (or the text in the middle of the screen) to start a new movie project. In future, your created projects will appear on this screen for you to select from, complete with details of their name and length. To delete a project, simply highlight it and tap the bin icon, bottom-right.

Step 2: Using The Undo Feature

Before you import anything into your project, it's important that you know about a very crucial function of iMovie: the undo feature. If you make a mistake or do something wrong, you can immediately reverse it by shaking your iPad and pressing 'Undo'. You can also do this to redo an action if you decide that you didn't want to undo what you undid after all.

Step 3: Adding Pre-Recorded Video

Once the timeline screen appears, tap the film/music icon on the left and you'll be taken to a library of all the videos currently stored on your iPad. To add one to your project, just tap it and press the blue arrow button that appears in the middle. You can also touch/drag the yellow dots on either end of each video snippet to only add a section of that video instead.

Step 4: Recording Video In iMovie

iMovie also gives you the option to record fresh video directly into the timeline. Tap the camera icon on the right and you'll get a similar display to the Camera app in video mode. After recording your video as normal, you can check it out using the play and timeline controls, then hit either 'Use' to import it into your project or 'Retake' to film a totally new video.

iPad mini

How To Use... iMovie (continued)

Step 5: Adding Photos To Your Project

Interestingly, you can also add stills photography to any iMovie project; perhaps you'll want to use one as a title screen or to help break up a particularly long scene. To do it, tap the film/music icon and then touch the photos button at the bottom of the page to reveal a similar interface to the Photos app. Tap the image you want, to then insert it into your project's timeline.

Step 6: Rearranging Video/Photo Clips

Your video and photo content will appear on the timeline screen at the bottom, and you can keep adding clips/photos until you've got everything you want to edit together. If you want to rearrange the clip/photo order, though, just touch and hold your finger on the one that you're moving, then drag it along the timeline to where you want it before or after another clip.

Step 7: Advanced Clip Rearranging

If you want to reposition a clip/photo into the middle of a clip rather than the beginning or end, you need to create a split point. Drag the red timeline at the bottom to exactly where you want the split to be and touch the clip to highlight it. Now swipe down with your finger quickly to cut the clip in half. This only works with video clips currently in the timeline, though, and not photos.

Step 8: Trimming Clip/Photo Length

Just as you did when you imported previously recorded video into your timeline, you can now trim down the length of your clips and photos by tapping the clip to highlight it, then dragging the yellow dots at the beginning and end inwards. The number shown indicating the clip length will decrease to compensate. When you're done, touch off the clip to deselect it.

iTip – USING LOCATION DATA
When you first open iMovie, be sure to say 'OK' if it asks to use your location data. If you don't, you won't be able to access videos or photos in your Camera Roll.

Step 9: Changing Project Settings

Tapping the cog button in the top-right corner brings up the Project Settings menu. The main setting is the theme, which sets the style of any theme music or subtitles you apply. Simply drag the small windows left and right to pick the one you want. You can also turn on theme music here and set your project to fade to/from black at the start or the end of it.

Step 10: Playing With Transitions

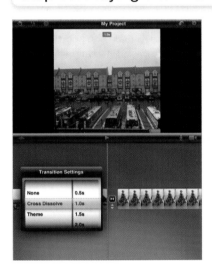

Any breaks sitting between clips are handled by transitions. Double-tap one of the black squares between clips/photos to access the settings for that transition; you can choose its length and set the style to match your chosen theme, be a simple cross-fade or do nothing. Each transition is unique, so you need to change the settings for each one individually.

Step 11: Editing Photo Clips

Imported photos are different to video clips; instead of playing, iMovie applies a movement effect called Ken Burns to make things more interesting. You can control this effect by tapping the photo, then dragging to change its position around and pinching to zoom in/out. Do this for the start and end to set positional markers and then iMovie fills in the blanks itself.

Step 12: Adding Captions And Locations

To add title captions to any clip, double-tap it to see the 'Clip Settings' menu. Touch 'Title Style', choose where the caption will appear (at the start, middle or end), then tap the 'Title Text Here' box and fill in what you want it to say. To add a location, just tap 'Location', and tap the target button to detect your current location or tap 'Other' and type it into the search box.

How To Use... iMovie (continued)

Step 13: Adjusting A Clip's Sound Levels

If you're currently viewing a video clip with sound attached, the 'Clip Settings' screen will also display a volume control slider. You can slide this to the left or right with your finger to decrease or increase the sound level of the clip, or just flick the switch to the off setting to remove the sound entirely. That's handy if you want any music to take precedence.

Step 14: Adding Your Own Music

Although you can apply generic music in the 'Project Settings' screen, you can also add your own music track from your tunes on your iPad. Touch the film/music icon on the timeline screen, then tap 'Audio'. Theme music and sound effects are provided by iMovie, while the other menus link to your music library. Just tap a song to add it to the timeline.

Step 15: Changing Music Sound Levels

As with the clip settings of video clips and photos, you can double-tap any added music track (which appear under the image timeline as a thin green bar) to bring up the 'Audio Clip Settings'. Obviously, the only thing you can change is the volume. Don't forget, added audio automatically fades when video audio is playing, unless you specifically set it not to.

Step 16: Deleting Clips And Audio

If you decide that you've added something that you now don't want, you can remove it by going into the clip settings for that section (double-tap the clip/photo/music track) and pressing the red 'Delete' button at the bottom. Remember: only do this if you're sure, because iMovie's undo option only undoes the last action you performed!

iTip – VIDEO EFFECT APPS AND iMOVIE
You can use any video effect app available in the App Store to create video clips that work in iMovie, as long as the app outputs the video into your Camera Roll folder.

Step 17: Adding A Voiceover Track

To add a voiceover, move the timeline to where you want it to start, then press the microphone button at the top. Hit the record button when you're ready, watch the countdown, then start talking as the video plays. Hit 'Stop' and you review what you did, discard and re-record it or keep the track. Voiceovers appear in the timeline as a purple bar to set them apart.

Step 18: Watching Your Edited Project

To see how your edited video is coming along, press the play button in the middle of the screen and it'll play from wherever you've set the timeline marker. Alternatively, press the star button in the top-left corner and then the play button on the 'Project' screen to have it play from the start in full-screen mode (with the iPad in landscape mode), as you would a normal movie.

Step 19: Finalising Your Project

Once you're happy with your video project, it's time to finish it off. Start by giving it a proper title. Hit the star button in the top-left corner of the timeline screen to return to the 'Projects' page, then tap the display where it says 'New Project'. This brings up the keyboard, so type in a name for your video that describes it best and then hit the 'Done' button to set it in place.

Step 20: Sharing Your Project

Now let's put your project where others can see it! Hit the arrow button at the bottom of the 'Projects' screen to see iMovie's various sharing options; you can save it to your Camera Roll or upload it to YouTube or Facebook (if you have accounts logged with your iPad) or even send it to iTunes, allowing you to pick up the project on an iPhone or iPod Touch.

iPad mini

Related Photography And Video Apps

Not surprisingly, photo and video apps on the iPad are ten a-penny but you really only need the best ones to make the most of your camera's creativity. Choose from colour effects and clip editing to crazy face changers and more besides…

Vapp

Price: Free
Developed By: O Street
In-app Purchases: No

Taking photos with an iPad can be a bit fiddly, because the tablet is such an unwieldly size, but Vapp might be able to help, since it uses sound as a trigger to take a photo. You can clap, tap, stamp or call out to your iPad to get it to take a picture. It's particularly useful for group photos, because it means no one has to hold the iPad to get the shot.

Videolicious

Price: Free
Developed By: The Talk Market
In-app Purchases: No

Ever wanted to make a great video clip but don't have a clue where to start? Well, don't worry; Videolicious does much of the work for you! Just choose the clips you want to include in your video, put them in order and add some music, then watch as the app builds a professional-looking video package automatically with no effort on your part. You can still claim all the credit, though…

WiFi Photo Transfer

Price: Free
Developed By: Voxeloid Kft.
In-app Purchases: No

It's fine being able to transfer your photos into your own copy of iTunes, but how about putting them on a computer you're not synced with? With this app, you can access all the photos on your iPad using the web browser of any computer. Just boot up the app and then enter the web address shown into the browser to have access to your entire library, ready to be downloaded.

Slow Shutter Cam

Price: £1.49 / $1.99
Developed By: Cogitap Software
In-app Purchases: No

The camera functions on the iPad are reasonably basic, which is no surprise given that most people will use it for little more than point-and-click photography and simple video capture. However, if you want to change the shutter speed of the built-in iSight and get some snazzy effects going in your photography, then this app will help you add varying degrees of motion blur to your images by slowing things way down.

Viddy

Price: Free
Developed By: Viddy Inc
In-app Purchases: Yes (music, etc.)

For moments when just taking a photo isn't enough. Viddy is all about taking short videos, editing them, and sharing them. The longest video you can take using the app is 15 seconds, so it really is all about capturing one moment in time, rather than making a whole film. There are plenty of free video effects and tools, and even more if you're willing to pay for them. It's also easy to share videos via Facebook, Twitter, YouTube, or Tumblr.

Color Effects

Price: Free
Developed By: Daniel Cota
In-app Purchases: Yes (remove adverts)

When it comes to getting dramatic effects for very little effort, it doesn't get much better (or cheaper, since it's totally free) than Color Effects. Use your finger to bring sections of your images to vivid life, leaving the rest black and white, then share your new creations immediately through Twitter and Facebook, save them to your Camera Roll for viewing later on or email your image to one of your contacts.

Snapseed

Price: £2.99 / $4.99
Developed By: Nik Software
In-app Purchases: No

Chances are you've heard of Instagram. It's part photo app, part social media network and has taken the pocket photography world by storm. Weirdly, though, there's no iPad version to speak of, so iPad owners have missed out on the phenomenon – at least, they had until Snapseed came along.

In stepping in to fill Instagram's iPad-sized shoes, Snapseed offers a wealth of options for the budding creative photographer. Editing-wise, you can choose from a wide range of different filter effects to give your images a real retro flavour or choose a narrow depth of focus where things in the center of your shot appear in sharp focus while those on the periphery are very blurred. What's more, all the effects can be applied to images either as you take them or retrospectively to images from your photo library.

As for the sharing element, it has the usual elements (Twitter, Facebook, Flickr), but it also has the bonus of linking directly to Instagram's social network gallery, which is a huge plus when the real app doesn't exist for iPad owners. By linking Snapseed to the Instagram network, it means your friends can follow your images and see your pictures as you post them through the app. You can also enable the geotagging function so you can see images that have been tagged as being near your current location as well. Looks like Instagram's developers have missed the boat then…

Pro HDR

Price: £1.49 / $1.99
Developed By: eyeApps LLC
In-app Purchases: No

Bizarrely, the iPad camera is missing one key option that the iPhone version has: you can't use it to take HDR (High Dynamic Range) photos. Thankfully, this clever and cheap app can provide the same function, allowing you to really maximise your photography with little fuss. Pro HDR, as with the HDR option on the iPhone, actually takes multiple photos at the same time, each one tuned to a specific element: highlights, shadows and so on. It then merges these photos together to capture the best of each element and helps you get a photo that really represents what you can see, rather than losing things like sky or foreground through a lack or excess of light.

VideoCam3D Lite

Price: Free
Developed By: NXP Software
In-app Purchases: No

The world of 3D video has come a long way in recent times thanks to handheld devices like the Nintendo 3DS, but there's still room for old-fashioned 3D effects too. Unlike new technology that allows you to see 3D without the need for glasses, VideoCam3D uses good old red and blue filters to separate video footage before letting you play it back in 3D – provided you have a pair of old-school 3D glasses to hand, that is. Not only can it record fresh video with the effect, but it can also be used to apply 3D effects retrospectively to videos that you've already recorded. You can then share your videos with your friends via Facebook or YouTube if you feel inclined.

Picframe

Price: £0.69 / $0.99
Developed By: David Boyes
In-app Purchases: Yes (image labels)

Picframe is a great little app that helps you to combine a number of photographs from your iPad into great-looking frame-style mosaics that you can then share via Facebook, Twitter, Flickr and Tumblr. There are a variety of different formats to choose between, with 34 different frames included as standard in the app, different patterns available for the external frame of the montage itself, as well as a changeable border width depending on how visible you want it to be. It's easy to use too. You simply drag and drop the images you want to include into the desired area in the frame. The effects can also be applied to individual photographs.

iPad mini

iMotion HD

Price: Free
Developed By: Fingerlab
In-app Purchases: Yes (export options)

Recording video with the iPad's camera isn't hard, but capturing something that could be considered genuinely great is a little more tough. And that's just regular 'point and shoot' video we're talking about; given by the amount of effort that it requires, you'd think that something super arty like stop-motion animation is incredibly difficult to do with an iPad, right? It would be if you didn't use iMotion HD.

This clever (and mostly free, save for the ability to export your videos being hidden behind an in-app purchase) app utilises two different video styles: time-

lapse and stop-motion. Using the first, you can capture video that looks like time has been accelerated – so, making clouds move faster across the sky, for example – while using the second can make inanimate objects look like they're moving on their own, much in the same way that Wallace & Gromit are brought to life. Stop-motion obviously requires a bit more planning and some input on your part, but iMotion HD takes a lot of the sting out of getting your ideas on video and can help you make something that looks professional thanks to its 720p HD output quality.

As mentioned though, the only real snag is with iMotion HD's sharing options: they're not there until you cough up £2 for the in-app purchase. To be fair, that's still a bargain for what you're getting, so we shouldn't be too cross about it…

ComicBook!

Price: £0.69 / $0.99
Developed By: 3DTOPO Inc
In-app Purchases: No

Ever wanted to star in your own comic book as a hero or villain? Well, now you can (kind of) with the ComicBook! photo app. It comes pre-loaded with over 50 different graphics and 30 layouts into which you can import photos, which you can then add filters, effects and other layers to in order to give them that unique comic book feel. You can also put speech bubbles onto your creations to literally put words into people's mouths and tell a story, as well as combine different elements of multiple photos to make the perfect scene. When you're done, everything can then be exported to Facebook or sent by email so that your friends can have a laugh too. Maybe.

Pocketbooth

Price: £0.69 / $0.99
Developed By: Project Box
In-app Purchases: Yes (effects, etc.)

If you've ever piled into a photo booth with your friends to take silly photos, you're going to love Pocketbooth, because this fun app is all about recreating that experience. You can take and edit photos using it, adding all kinds of retro effects to make your pictures look more like they came out of an authentic photo booth and you can even order printed out photo-strips of your pictures to be delivered to your doorstep. Because this is a modern app and not a creaky old photobooth, though, it can also export images to other digital formats and can add them to your social media account at the touch of a button.

Percolator

Price: £1.49 / $1.99
Developed By: Tinrocket
In-app Purchases: No

An app with an interesting take on the photo filter editing that takes up much of the Photography section of the App Store, Percolator offers you the chance to, er, percolate your photos. Much like coffee, you can filter your images and turn them into subtly coloured mosaics peppered with artistic bubbles. It sounds weird, but the effects are actually really tasteful and more than a little pretty. Also, it actively encourages you to use it in combination with other photo effect apps in order to get a truly unique result. With simple dial-based controls and a retro-style design that's as kitsch as it is classy, you'll probably enjoy using it far more than you'd expect.

Powercam HD

Price: Free
Developed By: Wondershare Software
In-app Purchases: No

While there are plenty of camera apps that can add a wide variety of effects to your photos, Powercam HD can also add the same effects (colour splash, tilt shift, vintage film and more) to your video recordings too. Thanks to its range of built-in social networking tools, it can also share your videos directly to a wide range of social media sites like Facebook, Twitter and YouTube.

Video Star

Price: £0.69 / $0.99
Developed By: Frontier Design Group
In-app Purchases: Yes (more effects)

Ever wanted to be the star of your very own music video? Then you're either a young girl or a bit odd. Either way, you'll want to get hold of Video Star – a beefed-up version of Video FX Live, reviewed on the right – which can take music from your iPad and then let you sing, dance and generally record yourself doing things to, before adding special effects and other editing techniques.

Video FX Live

Price: Free
Developed By: Frontier Design Group
In-app Purchases: Yes (more effects)

Where iMovie on iPad falls down is in the special effects department, mainly because it doesn't have any that you can apply to your recorded creations. However, you can use VideoFX Live to add all manner of effects to your video clips before you edit them together; you can even combine effects and colour styles to make your own crazy concoctions instead.

360 Panorama

Price: £0.69 / $0.99
Developed By: Occipital
In-app Purchases: No

Stitching together panoramic photographs with a basic camera can be a horribly arduous task that requires a reasonable amount of skill to get right, and lining things up and making it look right is usually more effort than it's worth. 360 Panorama, however, allows you to take a panoramic image using your iPad with a single button press and a steady hand. Simple to use, this app produces impressive results for little outlay.

Blurb Mobile

Price: Free
Developed By: Blurb Inc
In-app Purchases: No

If a picture tells a thousand words, what would several pictures and a heap of video clips all tied together with captions tell? A whole story, if Blurb is to be believed: this app lets you import your favourite photos and videos, set them to music and create your own stories that can then be shared with friends via Facebook, Twitter, Tumblr or email and has a story stream that people can follow for when you add new content.

Hipstamatic

Price: £0.69 / $0.99
Developed By: Hipstamatic LLC
In-app Purchases: Yes (unlock options)

With this app, you can apply all sorts of effects to make it look like your photos were taken on a real camera with an assortment of lenses, flashes, and film types to choose from. As you'd expect, you can instantly share your works of photographic art with your friends via all the usual social media platforms, and if you're really good, you can enter Hipstamatic's regular photography competitions to show off your skills.

iPad mini

Your iPad mini And...
Organisation

Are you anything like us? Do you struggle to remember birthdays? Do you find it hard to keep on top of where you've got to be and when? Could you sometimes use a helping hand to just keep your day-to-day life in track? If you are, then fortunately, help is very much at hand.

That's because built into the Apple iOS 6 operating system from the off is a welcome collection of tools that can help you keep your life in order. Furthermore, given the inherent portability of the iPad mini, it means you can have a sort-of personal assistant at hand whenever you need it!

What the iPad mini brings together then is actually a collection of really helpful little tools, which might not be massively sophisticated but which still prove to be remarkably helpful. Thus, there's the Calendar functionality, which acts as your own personal diary, to the point of reminding you when important events are coming up. You can also set up and customise notifications and prioritise them as well, and keep on top of key dates.

The Reminders system built into iOS 6 is surprisingly sophisticated, offering a number of different parameters that can trigger reminders based on a collection of criteria available for you to choose from.

Furthermore, if you're on the move and in something of a rush, why not take advantage of the dictation functionality that's built into your iPad mini?

However, the real gold where organisation is concerned comes in the App Store. A simple download such as Dropbox has proven to be a lifesaver, for example, for many people who want access to their documents wherever they happen to be. It's not the only high-quality tool that you might want to try either, and our round-up of useful apps at the end of the chapter is well worth checking out...

How To Use... Reminders

If you have a memory like a sieve can't remember anything without a little prompting, then the handy Reminders function on your iPad could really save your bacon...

Step 1: Create A Reminder

The Reminders app is pre-loaded on your iPad and appears on your home screen. Touch it to open it and you'll see a blank list. However, if you want to become super-organised, that list won't stay blank for long! Tap one of the lines to create your first reminder. The keyboard will appear and you can just type in whatever it is you need to remember.

Step 2: Make A List

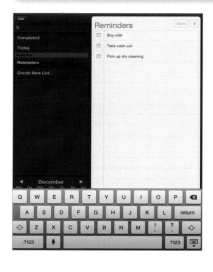

If you think you'll remember to check your reminders list regularly enough, that's all you need to do. You can just keep typing in your to-do list, save it, and refer back to it whenever is necessary. However, the point of a reminder is to, as you might expect, actually remind you. With that in mind, once you've entered your task, touch it to open up the 'Edit' menu.

Step 3: Set A Date

In the dialogue box that pops up, touch the slider next to 'Remind Me On A Day' and you can set a timed reminder. So if you need to remember to buy milk before your mum comes round, use the date sliders to enter a date and time. This can be as soon or as far in the future as you like. If there's no deadline, you can skip this step.

Step 4: Get A Regular Reminder

If the thing you need to remember is a regularly recurring event, such as an appointment or a birthday or perhaps a gym class, then you can use the Repeat function in the 'Reminders' menu so you don't have to keep entering it time after time. That way, your iPad will remind you every time this task is due. For anniversaries, this might be particularly helpful!

Step 5: Prioritise

When you have a long list of things that need doing, it can be hard to know where to start, but the Reminder app will let you assign each task a priority level. Tap 'Show More...' in the 'Edit' menu, then tap 'Priority' to tell the app whether your task is high, medium or low priority. You'll see a number of exclamation points beside the task which tells you how important it is!

Step 6: Feel A Sense of Accomplishment

When you've completed a task on your list, you just need to touch the box next to it on the 'Reminders' list to tick it off. If you pull the screen down, you'll see the number of tasks you've completed while you've been using Reminders, and if you touch the number you'll get a full list of everything you've crossed off your list. Feels good, doesn't it?

iPad mini

How To Use... Calendar

You can take your appointments book with you everywhere you go thanks to your iPad's built-in calendar. With the ability to remind yourself via alerts, you need never miss another meeting again

Step 1: Viewing Your Forthcoming Plans

Once you're in the Calendar app, you'll see that there are a number of choices about how you can view your upcoming plans – daily, monthly or as a list (shown here). The month view shows a dot beneath any day that has an appointment on, while the daily view breaks it into half-hour chunks. The list, meanwhile, shows appointments in date order.

Step 2: Making An Appointment

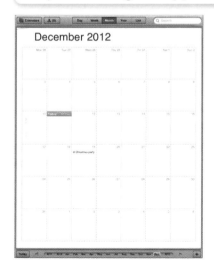

In the month view, you can move ahead to other months (and back again) using the arrows at the top of the calendar. The current date is shown with a blue bar, and pressing on another day will highlight that day in grey. Once you've selected the day to add an appointment to, touch the events list to open the option for adding a new event.

iTip – CALENDAR FUNCTIONALITY

Turn the iPad on its side while viewing the Calendar to get a more detailed day-by-day view that you can scroll through with your finger. Very handy indeed!

Step 3: Giving Your Event A Name

You can now name your event as a way of remembering what it is and add the location that it'll take place in. In our example, we have a meeting with Uncooked Media at Uncooked HQ. Whatever you type into the top box will be the 'name' of the event and is what will be displayed in your info box (should you set a reminder) and in the calendar, so you should make the name self-explanatory.

Step 4: Setting The Time Of Your Event

The box below enables you to set exactly when the event will be happening. By default, the date will match the one highlighted in your diary, but you can use the scroll wheels to change this, as well as setting a start and end time for your appointment. You can change the date on the end time if an event runs over more than one day, and the slider can indicate an all-day event.

Step 5: Setting Up A Repeating Event

It may be that you have a regularly recurring event and you don't want to have to enter each one separately. Selecting the 'Repeat' box gives you some pre-set repeat options for frequent meetings. Note that monthly repeats the meeting on the same date each month, rather than, for example, on the first Monday. The same applies for the yearly settings as well.

Step 6: Reminding Yourself Of Your Event

You can also tell Calendar what kind of notice you want of the meeting by selecting the 'Alert' box. You can choose to be reminded of your meeting either as it's due to start or at a variety of intervals beforehand. You can then set a second reminder nearer the time so you don't forget. You can save your reminder(s) for just this event or all events (if it's a recurring one).

iPad mini

How To Use... Notifications

A particularly useful feature in iOS 6 is the notifications panel. With one simple swipe of the phone, you can see the latest information from the apps you feel are most relevant to you

Step 1: What Is The Notifications Panel?

We won't assume you know how to get to the new notifications panel, because, believe it or not, many iPad mini users only find it by accident! Swiping your finger from the clock at the top of the screen brings the notifications panel down, showing you information from some of your apps. Think of it as a pull-down shutter over your display. You get rid of it by swiping upwards.

Step 2: Changing Notification Settings

So now we know what it is, how do we determine which apps are displayed in the notifications panel? It gives you immediate access to the latest updates from apps that you have selected, so only choose the most relevant apps. You can start that process by touching the Settings menu and then choosing the 'Notifications' section to bring up a list.

Step 3: Turning Notifications On/Off

Touch any of the items in the list and you'll be able to toggle notifications on and off. If you want them on, you can also set more detailed instructions. For example, you can choose how many items should be shown in the Notifications panel, whether info should appear as a banner, an alert or not at all, and whether they should pop up on the lock screen.

Step 4: Leave Me Alone

If you want to temporarily disable everything (say, if you have a meeting), you can set your iPad to 'Do Not Disturb' mode. This will silence all incoming alerts and calls. If you'd like to know if there's an emergency, though, you can set it so certain people are allowed to call or if someone makes repeated calls, they're allowed through. Just touch the buttons to enable these options.

How To Use... Dictation

Need to send a text but only have one hand (or even no hands) free? Don't feel like typing on a virtual keyboard? Then get Siri to do it for you. All you have to do is talk...

Step 1: Talk To Siri

You probably turned Siri on when you were setting up your iPad mini, but just in case you didn't, you can easily do it now. Open the Settings menu, touch 'General', and then tap 'Siri'. Toggle the switch to 'On'. Now, to get started talking to 'Siri', press and hold the home button on your iPad, and Siri will pop up in a new window to ask what it can help with.

Step 2: Make A Note

Siri can take dictation on pretty much anything you'd normally type; you just have to ask. Touch the microphone and ask Siri to take a new note by saying "Take a new note." Siri will respond by asking what you want the note to say, then just say whatever it is you want the note to say. It's really that simple. If you want to add punctuation, you can just say it as you go along.

Step 3: Send Tweets, Emails, And More

It's not just notes you can get Siri to take down for you. You can also ask it to send a tweet, email or message. Depending on what you're sending, you may need to add a recipient or a subject line, but Siri will ask you for that information as you go along, and you just need to tap the microphone button before replying to make sure that Siri is actually listening.

Step 4: Check What You're Sending

Siri is pretty good at understanding dictation, but it isn't always perfect, especially when it comes to words that sound identical, like 'whether' and 'weather'. Before sending anything, you should probably take a moment to check and correct anything that Siri has written for you, to avoid any misunderstandings cropping up.

iPad mini

Related Organisation Apps

If you want to keep yourself even better organised while on the go, then these apps are the ones for you. With this little lot, you'll really have no excuses for being late or missing an appointment ever again…

Dropbox

Price: Free
Developed By: Dropbox Inc
In-app Purchases: Yes (Increased storage)

The Dropbox app is basically identical to the 'big' computer version, enabling you to store folders in an online space and work across different computers (like home and work). This allows you to then access, upload and download files on the move, meaning you can work on your files wherever you are. You'll need to install it on your computer as well though to make it work properly…

Errands To-Do List

Price: Free
Developed By: David Mandell
In-app Purchases: Yes

This incredibly easy-to-use task manager app gives you a great deal of flexibility to categorise your jobs in a way that suits you, which is great if you need to keep yourself organised. You can assign them to folders; give them high, medium, low or no priority; create alarms; and set repeating events for things like 'the first Monday of the month', which the built-in Calendar can't do. Take that, Apple!

Clipbox

Price: £0.69 / $0.99
Developed By: haha Interactive
In-app Purchases: No

Always find yourself having flashes of brilliance but no way to keep everything together? Then you need Clipbox, an app that's essentially all those boxes in your garage that you've never got around to unpacking. Import text and photos, add tags to them to show what they are, collect them into boxes and them keep them safe while sharing over the cloud. Sounds pretty great, right?

Shift Worker

Price: £1.49 / $1.99
Developed By: Production Shed Pty Ltd
In-app Purchases: No

If you work unusual hours, it can be a hassle keeping track of them and even more of a hassle keeping other people in your life up to date on when you'll be working. Shift Worker is an organisation app aimed squarely at – you guessed it – shift workers. It lets users quickly and easily enter their work patterns and then share them via email, Facebook, Twitter, and messages. You can also add colour-coded notes to each shift.

Due

Price: £2.99 / $4.99
Developed By: Phocus LLP
In-app Purchases: No

While Calendar and Reminders are fairly slow-paced apps that want you to take your time in setting up those alarms, Due is all about speed. Need to set up a reminder in a flash? Use Due. Don't want the hassle of setting start or end times? Use Due. Don't even want to categorise your alarm? Use Due. Claiming to be up to three times faster than Apple's apps, this is one for those people who are too busy to have time to be busy.

Dragon Dictation

Price: Free
Developed By: Nuance Communications
In-app Purchases: No

Voice recognition software is all the rage right now, and if you have a new iPad, you'll even have Dictation built straight into the device. Still, Dragon has been doing it longer than anyone. This very accurate app allows you to dictate directly to your iPad, after which you can then amend any errors and send straight to email, text message, Facebook or Twitter. Has it become obselete, though? Well, only on the new iPad so far…

Evernote

Price: Free
Developed By: Evernote
In-app Purchases: Yes (monthly or annual subscription)

When it comes to organisation, Evernote is one of the most powerful tools available to keep your thoughts and documents in order, helping you to retrieve relevant information quickly and easily while also being ridiculously simple to use.

Unlike other organisers that tend to use text alone, Evernote allows you to save 'notes' as images, text, web clippings and audio files, then enables you to tag them as you see fit to help you remember what each one is for (and also make them searchable if you forget something later on). You can also access your Evernote account from any web browser and other iOS devices you might own (such as an iPhone), so you can get to your notes from pretty much anywhere.

The images that you store can even be searched thanks to some excellent text recognition software that really takes the whole app to another level. If a word appears in one of your images, then searching for that word will return a hit against that image - an advanced bit of coding that means Evernote is really the only note-taking application you will ever need. The icing on the cake is the fact that the interface is intuitive and easy to use. It really is a joy to behold.

To unleash the full power of Evernote on iPad, you can subscribe on a monthly or yearly basis (which is a little bit on the pricey side, if you ask us), but even the free basic version is streets ahead of the competition.

Air Sharing

Price: £5.49 / $7.99
Developed By: Avatron Software
In-app Purchases: No

Using iTunes to sync and add/remove files to your iPad is fine and dandy, but it can be a hassle if you don't have the cable to hand or, worse, aren't near a computer that your iPad is properly synced to (because we all know the horror of plugging in, then accidentally wiping all of our iPad's contents, right?). This simple app, however, enables the user to easily copy files between an iPad and a wirelessly connected Mac (either desktop computer or laptop). It means you can simply drag and drop your files on your Mac into the Air Sharing folder and then access them remotely from your iPad, making it easier than ever to work while you're on the move.

Remember The Milk

Price: Free
Developed By: Remember The Milk
In-app Purchases: Yes (Upgrade to Pro)

Remember The Milk is one of the most popular organisation apps, and for good reason: it's simple to use and syncs across every device you use, so you'll never have an excuse to forget anything ever again. You can create to-do lists with tags, locations, and priorities attached and sort them by any of that info to make sure you're getting things done in the most efficient way. It works even if you don't have an active connection: it'll just wait until you have to sync your info again. Although the app is free, you'll need to shell out for the Pro subscription to really get the best out of it. That costs £25 a year and adds extra features including push notifications and badges.

Corkulous Pro

Price: £2.99 / $4.99
Developed By: Appigo
In-app Purchases: No

Whereas most reminder-based apps are designed for use by just one person, Corkulous Pro actively encourages use by an entire group of people like a family or a business. Use the app to create a collective cork board, then invite other people by sharing that board through Dropbox and have them add their own notes to it with comments, reminders, ideas and other stuff. It's great for brainstorming and even better if you're trying to organise a family event or keep tabs on what the kids are meant to be doing (although, if we're honest, there's no way we'd let our kids loose with our iPads). It works with iCloud too, which makes sharing easier than ever.

Your iPad mini And...
Communication

No, it's not a phone; that's why the iPhone exists. However, even though it lacks the key component that makes the iPhone into a portable communication device (well, that and it's a bit bigger), that doesn't mean that the iPad mini can't be used to keep in touch with people. In fact, the iPad can do absolutely everything that the iPhone can do as far as communication goes aside from the telephone component. Even then, you can get apps that bypass that problem too.

Of course, Apple's iPhone has changed the landscape of portable communication forever which, in turn, means the iPad has also benefitted from the effect it's had. Just as the iPhone isn't just a phone, the iPad isn't just a tablet computer and entertainment device; it's also a portable means of communicating in pretty much every way possible. Put simply, it's a complete multimedia message centre. It

has the ability to send photos and videos to your friends; you can use it to instant message someone and get an immediate reply; send emails and stay in touch with the office, even when you're 100 miles from it; and use social networking like Facebook and Twitter, the latter of which is built directly into the back-end of the iPhone software. You can even chat face to face with people using video conferencing, something that never really seemed possible on a portable device until very recently. And that's before you consider all the communication apps available too, ranging from obvious ones like social network gadgets and media sharing to learning foreign languages or even knowing what each flag means in semaphore.

Seriously, who needs a phone when the iPad mini can give you so much more?

iPad mini

How To Use... Messages

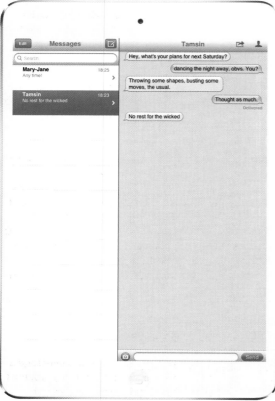

iMessage lets you send short, free messages to your friends' iOS devices, falling somewhere between the more personal phone call and the direct-but-impersonal email...

Step 1: The Message Inbox

Open the Messages app to see an empty screen with 'Messages' at the top. This is where all your conversations will eventually be stored. Of course, it'll be empty if you haven't used your iPad mini to send any messages before. The small pen and paper button in the top-right corner opens the 'New Message' screen, where you can send a message to someone.

Step 2: Adding Recipients To Messages

Touch the 'To:' bar and use the keyboard to enter the number of who the message is for. If their details are already in your contacts list, type the first few letters of their name to automatically bring up the names and numbers of people that match. Press the plus (+) button to bring up your whole contacts list. You can also enter multiple names to message several people.

iTip – DELETING MESSAGES
To delete messages, use the Edit button on the Message library to select multiple messages or swipe your finger over an individual message and press the Delete button.

Step 3: Adding Text & Sending A Message

Now tap the rounded bar above the keyboard to enter some message text. The iPad has no character limit on text messages, but your service provider may charge you for two or more messages if you write a lot of text, so try to keep it short. When you're done, simply hit 'Send' to send your message and store a copy in your message library for reference.

Step 4: Predictive Text And Corrections

The iPad loves predictive text and grammar correction, so don't be surprised when it tries to preempt or correct words, and check your text when you're done to make sure it's right! If there's an error, touch and hold down on a word to select and correct it. Touching and holding on a word also lets you find suggested words or tell you what its dictionary definition is.

Step 5: Adding Photos And Videos

To add a photo or video, tap the camera button on the left. You'll get the option to take a photo or video immediately (refer to pages 122 and 128 for more on doing that) or add one from your Camera Roll or Photo Stream. Do be aware, though, that large files will take a long time to send, so trying to send someone a video might not be a good idea.

Step 6: Deleting Messages

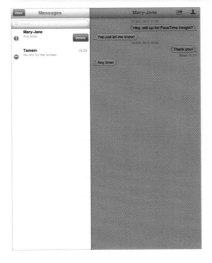

If you use iMessage a lot (and why wouldn't you?) you might find that your inbox gets pretty cluttered. There's a quick way to delete threads: just tap the 'Edit' button on the upper-left side of the screen and red buttons will appear beside each conversation. Touch it and a 'Delete' button will appear. Just press it to erase the conversation from your iPad mini.

How To Use... FaceTime

The iPad mini is really too big to use as a phone, but for FaceTime video calls, it's perfect. Just make sure you've tidied up before calling your mum...

Step 1: Finding FaceTime On Your iPad

FaceTime is built into the Phone app on an iPhone, but on the iPad it's a separate app. You'll find the icon on your home screen (or possibly in a folder, if you've tidied it away!). To get started making a call, just touch the icon. Note, though, that you'll need a Wi-Fi connection for it to work. Due to the data required, proper 3G and 4G support is still in its infancy.

Step 2: Limitations Of FaceTime Calling

The other limitation to be aware of, before you get started, is that the person you're calling will also need to have a) their own iOS device with FaceTime and b) a Wi-Fi connection to hand. This means FaceTime calls usually need to be arranged in advance to ensure that both people are able to connect, which makes it sound like quite a hassle, but being able to see who you're talking to makes it worth the effort.

iTip – 3G/4G FACETIME
As support for FaceTime over 3G and 4G networks is rolled out, do beware that it'll gobble up lots of your data allowance.

Step 3: Using FaceTime

In order to make a FaceTime call, you'll need to set it up with your email address. Go into Settings and choose 'FaceTime', Make sure the FaceTime option is on and the Apple ID is correct, then enter an email address as your contact details for FaceTime. Give this to people you want to FaceTime with and store their details in your contacts list. Now pick a person to call.

Step 4: Get Connected

Now open the FaceTime app and you'll see a list of all your contacts. Touch any of the names and you'll open a tab of information about them, which includes all their contact details and all the different ways you can contact them. Save emailing them for later, though, and hit the blue camera icon to make a FaceTime call. If they're available, you'll soon see their face popping up on your screen.

Step 5: In-call Controls

While you're in a FaceTime call, you'll see your own face in a smaller box in the corner. That little box lets you see what the other person is seeing, so you can make sure you keep that heap of laundry out of the shot! By default, FaceTime uses the front camera, but you can swap to the back camera by touching the flip icon. There's also an option to mute your mic.

Step 6: Say Goodbye

Now you're connected, you can chat to your heart's content. Video calls may never have become as popular as sci-fi predicted, but if you're talking to faraway friends, it's great to be able to see them and their surroundings! Stay within reach of your Wi-Fi connection, though, or you may find your call will disconnect. To hang up, just hit the 'End' button.

iPad mini

How To Use... Mail

The iPad is a great way to keep in touch - and the Mail app is just one more way to send and receive messages...

Step 1: Choosing Your Mail Provider

Interestingly, Apple has made the iPad's Mail app as all-encompassing as possible by making it compatible with a huge number of email services including Gmail, Microsoft Exchange, Yahoo!, Hotmail and more. You need to already have a suitable email account first, because only Apple's iCloud service lets you sign up directly through the iPad.

Step 2: Setting Up Your Account

Go to the Settings menu and select 'Mail', 'Contacts', 'Calendars', then choose 'Add Account'. Pick your service provider from the fairly extensive list provided and then enter your login details for that account. Once the iPad has verified your information, it'll sync up with your mail server and will be ready to go. You can then add more email accounts – as many as you like, in fact!

iTip – DELETING EMAIL ACCOUNTS
To delete an account from your iPad, go to Settings > Mail,
Contacts, Calendars > Accounts and hit Delete Account.
You can add it again later if you need to.

Step 3: Using Other Service Providers

Of course, it may be you're using an email provider that isn't listed on your iPad mini by default. In that case, scroll to the bottom of the list and pick 'Other'. Tap 'Add Mail Account' and then enter your login details for the account as before. Mail works with most POP- and IMAP-based mail servers, but check with your service provider if it doesn't work properly.

Step 4: Tweaking Your Settings – Push

First, let's play with the email settings. Select 'Mail', 'Contacts', 'Calendar' from the Settings menu, then touch 'Fetch New Data'. Ideally, you want 'Push' to be turned on, as this makes your mail server 'push' new emails to your iPad as they arrive in your server inbox. If you're going away, though, you should remember to turn it off to help keep your phone bills down.

Step 5: Tweaking Your Settings – Mail

The next batch of settings, under the heading 'Mail', are all about personal preference. Increasing the number of emails to store on your phone, reducing the font size, sending yourself copies of mail – it's all to be found here. You can also change the signature sent with all emails, since the default signature gives away that you're mailing from your iPad.

Step 6: Tweaking Your Settings – Accounts

Finally, scroll to the top and touch your email account under 'Accounts' for one last setting: with Archive Messages, you can choose to either permanently delete or save emails to your 'All Mail' folder from your phone with the on/off switch. Remember, though: delete means delete! Be absolutely sure before you set it to remove your emails for good.

How To Use... Mail (continued)

Step 7: Viewing Your Account – Multiple

When you actually open the Mail app, what you see depends on what you've already set up. The screen shown here on the left is based on an iPad with multiple email accounts working on it. You can opt to view all the inboxes at once, view them separately or see a detailed version of each account. If you only have one email account, what you'll end up seeing instead is...

Step 8: Viewing Your Account – Single

... this screen here, which is a similar detailed version of your account that multi-account users can access by choosing one in the 'Accounts' panel. From here, you can see everything: your inbox, any half-written drafts saved, emails sent and anything that's been moved to one of the various labeled folders. Simply touch any folder to open it up and see the contents.

Step 9: Viewing Your Inbox

Touching 'Inbox' shows you a list of emails currently in your inbox. Unread emails will have a blue marker by them on the left. Multiple emails in the same chain are indicated by a number on the right, holding everything inside a single notification. If you touch the single email shown in the inbox, you'll open another page showing you all the emails in the conversation.

Step 10: Searching Inboxes And Servers

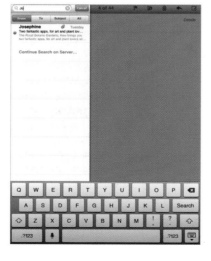

To search for a specific email, touch the search bar at the top and type something from it such as a name or a keyword, using the From/To/Subject/All buttons to say what part of the email it relates to. Anything relevant in your inbox will be shown in a list. If it's not on your phone, touch 'Continue Search On Server' to search your mail server and find a match.

iTip – ACCESSIBLE EMAIL FUNCTIONS
The buttons to check email and create a new email are easy to access, as they're on every page in the bottom-left and –right corners.

Step 11: Reading, Deleting And Archiving

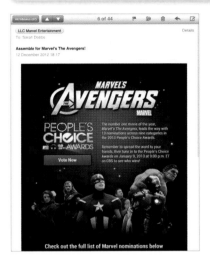

To open an email, touch it and then drag up or down with your finger to scroll through it; you can also use the pinch motion to zoom in/out. The middle three buttons on the blue bar at the bottom are shortcuts – use them to save the email to a folder, delete/archive it (depending on the settings you chose earlier on) or send a reply to one or all of the people on the email.

Step 12: Checking Contact Details

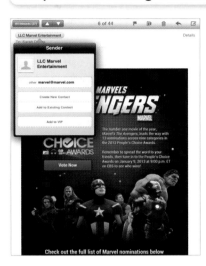

If you touch one of the blue email addresses at the top of any email, you can expand the name into a contact page. You can then save the email address to your contacts, either as a completely new contact or as an addition to one you already have. If it's already linked to a contact, you can send that person messages, call or Facetime with them instead.

Step 13: Sending Emails - Recipients

Press the pencil button in the top-right corner of the screen and you'll get the 'New Message' template. To add a recipient, either touch the plus button to see your contacts or type the name in directly. If you've sent emails from your iPad before, then a list of names will appear matching the letters that you type. You can add as many names to an email chain as you like.

Step 14: Sending Emails – Sending

Entering text into the subject header and email body is simply a matter of touching the screen to move the cursor and then typing. Anything you type can be tapped to select and correct/delete quickly. When you're done, just touch the 'Send' button to send it or you can press 'Cancel' and either save what you've written already as a draft or discard it completely.

iPad mini

How To Use... Twitter Through iOS 6

Why bother installing an additional app to do your social networking? iOS 6 has Twitter built straight into a wide range of pre-loaded apps, which makes things so much easier!

Step 1: Linking Your iPad To Twitter

iOS 6's integration of Twitter lets you to tweet photos, web pages, videos and locations directly from the other iPad apps. To link your iPad to your Twitter account, go to Settings and select 'Twitter', then press 'Add Account' to either input your username/password or create a new account. You can also add multiple Twitter accounts to a single iPad.

Step 2: Tweeting From Within Apps

From within the Photos, Safari or YouTube apps, put what you want to tweet on screen and press the curved arrow button. Several options will appear including 'Tweet'. Press this and enter any additional comments before hitting 'Send'. Note that attachments take up some of your 140-character limit, so don't write too much extra text in your tweet!

Step 3: Adding Location Info To Tweets

If you want, you can also include your current location on the bottom of your tweet. Just touch the 'Add Location' marker at the bottom of the Twitter panel and the iPad's GPS tracker will take care of the rest. However, Twitter has to be activated in your Location Services before this will work. You'll find Location Services in the Settings menu, so make sure you turn it on!

Step 4: Using Maps To Tweet Locations

Using the Maps app to share location details is a little different. Search for your location as normal and either touch the pin or drop a new pin to show the info panel. Touch 'Share Location' and then choose 'Tweet' to bring up a Twitter panel as normal. However, because you're linking to a map location, you can't add another location to the tweet as before.

Twitter

Price: Free
Developed By: Twitter
In-App Purchases: No

When you're busy, sometimes you'll only have time to put your thoughts into 140 characters or less. Thank heavens for Twitter then, where short bursts of text are par for the course…

We'll be the first to admit that when it comes to social networking, we always used to think that Twitter was the last thing we'd get into. Why bother with having to come up with abbreviated versions of what you're really thinking when you can say everything you want on Facebook in full? Why should I care about what some random person that I've never met before is doing right this second? Do I really need to know that you're going to the toilet/you're on the toilet/you've just been to the toilet? Seeing as you were busy tweeting, you probably didn't even wash your hands! Yep, as far as we were concerned, Twitter was pointless.

> Having such a social portal in the palm of your hand is a veritable godsend, especially if you happen to use Twitter as more than just a means of telling everyone what you had for breakfast

Or at least, that was until we actually got on there and started using it to share our thoughts and actions.

What followed was a weird transformation, an almost sideways shift as we moved away from posting status updates on Facebook and instead coming up with clever comments to fit inside Twitter's oh-so-tight limit on how much you say. Believe it or not, but writing something insightful, thought-provoking or just plain funny in just 140 characters (including spaces and punctuation!) isn't as easy as it looks. Thankfully, most of the people we follow - famous witty folk like Stephen Fry and Peter Serafinowicz - have it down to a tee. Us, though? We just talk about biscuits and complain about the weather most of the time, with blinding moments of insight coming as rarely as hell freezes over. That's still pretty rare, right?

Of course, that's part of the charm of Twitter. You can say pretty much whatever you like, spend your time trying to amass a collection of followers that would make the Chinese army look

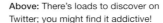

Above: There's loads to discover on Twitter; you might find it addictive!

Above: You can add photos directly into your tweets, which is handy.

positively tiny and generally marvel over what other people have to say, wishing that you'd been smart enough to say it first (and then either retweeting said clever words or, if you're less honest, tweeting them as your own and not saying you stole it). The trick lies in following the right people, reading the right web links, retweeting (read: forwarding on) the right comments and replying to the right tweets (read: posts). Thankfully, actually doing those things - following, retweeting, replying, tweeting - is incredibly easy on a computer, since you just click the relevant button on screen. And on the iPad? Well, it's even easier still.

Of course, putting Twitter on your iPad is just asking for trouble if you're easily distracted. It means that wherever you are, whatever you're doing, you have the ability to share your actions with the world (or your followers, at least). Equally, having such a social portal in the palm of your hand is a veritable godsend, especially if you happen to use Twitter as more than just a means of telling everyone what you had for breakfast. In the Twitter world, retweets and followers are everything, mentions and interactions are proof that you're popular, and hashtags are a means of getting yourself noticed the world over. And that, dear friends, is the kind of publicity that money can't buy. Well, not unless you have a lot of it anyway.

Still, the question remains: with so many different Twitter-enabled apps available for the iPad, why should you bother with the official one? Well, besides the fact that it's free, it also follows the pattern of being the best one, because it's made by Twitter itself. It rarely goes wrong (if ever), offers all the features of the full-fat computer version and more besides (multiple accounts without the need to sign in/out!), it's ridiculously simple to use and generally works a treat, which is all we ask of something that we've become horribly addicted to since installing it. Surely that's enough of a reason, eh?

How To Use... Twitter

The built-in Twitter mechanics of iOS are very useful, but they're not the whole Twitter experience. For that, you need to get your hands on the proper Twitter app instead. Here's how it works…

Step 1: Downloading The Twitter App

Common sense would suggest that you're best off going to the App Store and downloading the Twitter app from there, but you're wrong; it's actually far easier to go into Settings, selecting 'Twitter' from the menu and then pressing the 'Install' button at the top of the screen. This way, you can't accidentally download an unofficial app instead.

Step 2: Setting Up Your Account

If you already have a Twitter account and have followed the steps to connect to your iPad through iOS 6 then the Twitter app will automatically log you in. If not, you'll need to press the plus button to add an account to the app. Type your username and password into the respective fields and press 'Save' to log in. It'll be stored for future use as well.

iTip – USING HASHTAGS
Create a hashtag reference by typing '#' and then putting anything you like. You can't include spaces, punctuation or capital letters, though, or they won't work properly.

Step 3: Using The Twitter Feed

The first page you should see is marked 'Home' on the control bar at the bottom. This is your main Twitter feed and shows every update from every person that you're following. Touch any tweet to see extra buttons letting you reply, retweet, favourite and copy/email the tweet. You can also then touch the name/icon of the tweeter to see their full Twitter profile.

Step 4: Know Your Pages

Also on the bottom are 'Connect', 'Discover' and 'Me'. 'Connect' is where you'll see all the tweets replying to your own or mentioning your username (plus people who started following you). 'Discover' shows topics that are currently popular on Twitter that match those on your Twitter feed. Finally, 'Me' is your profile page with access to direct messaging.

Step 5: Sending A Tweet

Every page of the Twitter app has a quill button in the top-right corner. Pressing this brings up a text entry screen, allowing you to use the keyboard to type out your tweet. When you're completely happy with what you've written, just press the 'Tweet' button and it should then appear on your Twitter feed (and that of your followers) in mere seconds.

Step 6: Added Extras

You can reference people in a tweet by pressing the '@' button and then either picking their username from the list or typing it in, add a photo with the camera button or post your location by touching the arrow button. You can even create your own hashtags. Touch the '#' button and then either pick from the list or type anything you want without spaces.

Facebook

Price: Free
Developed By: Facebook
In-App Purchases: No

It may not have been the first social network, but by golly it's the biggest now. That means if you're not part of the Facebook community, you're missing out. Especially on the iPad mini…

You only have to look at the numbers to see that Facebook's popular these days. Indeed, thinking about it, we can only really think of a tiny handful of people we know who aren't on Facebook, and that's really only because they're massive technophobes who think that computers are evil. Apart from that, though, this really is the Facebook generation. Even our parents and grandparents are on there and many of them aren't great with computers. That's got to say something, right?

> Want to use it for interesting social means like building awareness for a business, brand or new product? You can do that

Of course, the chances are that if you're interested enough to own an iPad, then you probably have a Facebook account. What you use it for is really your business, though, because social networking's funny like that; it really is all down to interpretation. Want to use it for interesting social means like building awareness for a business, brand or new product? You can do that. Prefer to have Facebook help you keep tabs on long-lost friends, organise reunions with the people you went to school, college or university with and generally stay a part of their lives? You can do that too. Cataloguing your life, creating photo albums that tell a story like the development of your children or family, playing any number of the Facebook-specific social games that can totally drain your life - it's all possible.

In any case, Facebook can be a great thing; the only problem originally was that you had to be near a computer to use it, which either meant that a) you'd be sitting in front of a computer instead of doing stuff that you could be talking about on Facebook, or b) you'd be wasting time at work and potentially getting into trouble since many firms now track what people are using their office PCs for. Once the tablet revolution hit, though, all bets were off. A portable version of Facebook you can take anywhere and use at any time? That's possibly the best thing ever… assuming you like Facebook, that is.

Above: Profile pages now match the new Timeline style of the main site.

Above: Pulling out this **handy side bar lets you navigate with ease.**

Even better, the iOS version of Facebook has come an incredibly long way since it first appeared. Previously, a simplified version of the full-fat social network, now the Facebook app offers pretty much everything that the main website does and even does it in a way that makes it more accessible and easier to use. Shortcut icons make it a piece of cake to check your friend requests, messages and recent notifications, while clearly labeled buttons pave the way for instant updates to your status or quick uploads of photos from where you are right now. Want to reply to someone's post? Tap a button and type. Want to filter your news feed according to time or popularity? Tap another button. Even sorting through all the different pages of Facebook has been made easy thanks to the addition of a collapsible sidebar that holds every link you could ever need – pages, apps, favourites and more besides. You can get push notifications in your Notifications panel, so you'll never miss a comment, Like or private message again. In iOS 6, Apple found new ways to integrate Facebook with other functions, which means it's easier to use, has more features and it's harder than ever to get away from!

Granted, it's not the best app in the world, because we can appreciate that not everyone's a Facebook fan. Some people refuse to use it because of privacy concerns, others hate the way it constantly feels the need to reinvent itself or the way it looks

> Even better, the iOS version of Facebook has come an incredibly long way since it first appeared

and works. However, if you are a fan and need Facebook in your life like smokers need cigarettes, then it's an essential download for your iPad, especially since it's totally free.

How To Use... Facebook

The iPad mini version of Facebook offers the same level of functionality as the main website. Thankfully, that doesn't make it any less portable!

Step 1: Download And Log In

Like Twitter, Facebook is integrated into iOS 6, so you can just go to the Settings menu to install the Facebook app or you can get it from the App Store. Load it up, and then enter your login email and password to get started. You can also sign up if you haven't already, but that works through a web browser rather than via the app.

Step 2: Check Your Settings

Some Facebook settings are available via the general Settings menu: you can decide whether or not chat and message alerts play sound, for instance. More detailed settings are available inside the Facebook app itself, including privacy and security settings; you'll find those by scrolling to the bottom and touching 'Account Settings' in the app. Now, it's time to fire up the app itself...

Step 3: This Is The News

Once you're in, you'll see the main news feed page; it's pretty much identical to the one you'd see on the proper version of Facebook, except trimmed to remove the superfluous bits like ads and birthday alerts. Drag your finger vertically up and down the screen to scroll through the updates or touch 'Sort' to arrange them by popularity or most recent posts.

Step 4: If It's Blue, It's Important

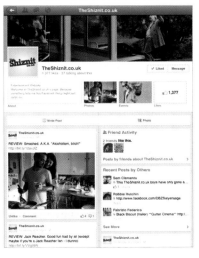

The important thing to remember about iPad Facebook, as with regular Facebook, is that anything appearing in blue on the screen is interactive. Clicking on the names of people in your news feed takes you to their profile page. Links to videos or external sites will also be displayed in blue, as will any options to expand posts that are overly long (labeled 'See More...' under the post).

iPad mini

How To Use... Facebook (continued)

Step 5: Liking And Commenting

If you want to interact with other people's posts, then you have two options. You can either 'like' what they've posted on Facebook, which just means hitting the 'Like' link under their post to register your approval and let them know you've seen it or you can leave a more detailed comment (just hit the 'Comment' link and type whatever it is you want to say).

Step 6: Shortcuts To Success

The icons in the blue bar at the top are your main notification shortcuts. Touching the two heads brings up a list of any outstanding friend requests that you've been sent (not that you've sent yourself), while the speech bubbles show a list of all your messages. Finally, the globe shows notifications of new comments following posts or comments of your own.

Step 7: Updating Your Status

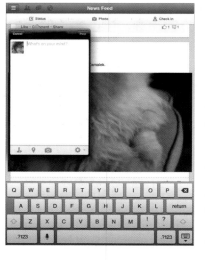

Since status updates are so important to Facebook, it makes sense that adding new ones would be easy. Just press the 'Status' button near the top of the screen and then type away. Unlike Twitter, there's no character limit (within reason, that is). Once you're happy with your update, touch the 'Post' button and it'll be uploaded onto Facebook immediately.

Step 8: Adding Photos And Locations

Although there are separate buttons for photo uploads and location check-ins, you can do both from the 'Update Status' area. Touch the camera icon to add a picture from your photo library or take a new one, or the inverted teardrop to add your location (although Facebook's location services have to be turned on in Settings for this to work).

iTip – REFRESHING THE NEWS FEED
To check for new posts on your news feed, scroll to the top and drag it down with your finger until Release To Update appears and it'll search for any updates.

Step 9: The Navigation Bar

Touching the three horizontal lines in the top-left corner of most (but not all) pages opens the hidden navigation bar. From here, you can access more detailed parts of Facebook such as your friends list, any events you're attending, your photos, any pages or groups that you like and so on. Just touch one of the headings and you'll be taken straight to the relevant page.

Step 10: Advanced Photo Uploading

Choosing 'Photos' from the navigation bar gives you greater control over your photo uploading. You can still choose to upload photos from your iPad library or take a new one using the iPad's camera, but you can also create new albums or add new pictures to current ones as well. Tap a picture to tag people in it or tap the grey bar to add a caption, then hit 'Upload'.

Step 11: Private Messaging

To send private messages, choose 'Messages' from the navigation bar and then press the pencil button in the top-right corner; type the name of the person or people you're sending it to or touch the plus button for a full list of friends. If you're replying to a received message, though, you can just type in the text panel at the bottom of the screen and hit 'Send'.

Step 12: Search For New Friends

The navigation bar has one more helpful tool: a search bar. Typing names into this (of real people, businesses, brands or anything else likely to have a presence on Facebook) brings up a list of relevant pages and people to choose from. It also shows you which search results your friends have in common with you, making it easier to see which might be the one you're looking for.

Related Communication Apps

Communicating isn't just about words, you know. From talking on the phone for free and learning a new language to chatting on forums and even meeting a new love, it's so much more when you have an iPad…

Talkatone

Price: Free
Developed By: TalkMe.IM Inc
In-App Purchases: Yes (subscriptions)

Unlike the more popular and well-known Skype (which we've covered just across the page), Talkatone is unique in that it doesn't require both ends of a conversation to have the software installed. That means that you can use your iPad as a phone to call pretty much anyone, although there's no denying that the fairly hefty subscription fees charged to do so make it a bit less enjoyable.

Find My Friends

Price: Free
Developed By: Apple
App Purchases: No

Okay, so knowing where everyone you know is at any time may seem a little controlling, but it actually has its benefits if, say, you're waiting for someone to turn up and want to see if they're late or just hiding. Using Find My Friends makes it totally possible, though; simply install the app on two iOS devices, accept an invite to follow each other and track away. Mmm, now that's good stalking.

Zoosk

Price: Free
Developed By: Zoosk Inc
App Purchases: Yes (membership, coins)

Ah, Internet dating: isn't it great? It's also the future of relationships (trust us, we've checked on that), so if you're looking for love through your iPad, look no further than Zoosk. The app is an extension of the website and can be used to send messages, check out singles and even find a partner. You have to be a member of Zoosk to use it, of course, but that's the price of love.

WhatsApp

Price: £0.69 / $0.99
Developed By: WhatsApp Inc
App Purchases: No

WhatsApp is a cross platform messenger that lets you talk to your friends for free. As well as sending instant text messages, you can send pictures and voice messages, and even set up group chats so you can talk to multiple people on multiple devices, all at the same time. You don't even need to set up another account, since WhatsApp works with your phone number and uses your existing contacts.

WordPress

Price: Free
Developed By: Automattic
App Purchases: No

Anyone who's anyone these days has their own website, and most people seem to plump for WordPress because it's so easy to use. This app also makes WordPress super portable, since it allows you to edit and manage your WordPress-created website from the comfort of your iPad – handy if you're out and about but suddenly have a flash of inspiration for a new blog post. Plus, like WordPress, it's totally free!

TOTALe Course HD

Price: Free
Developed By: Rosetta Stone
App Purchases: No

Okay, so the fact you have to own a full version of Rosetta Stone for your computer and a paid-up subscription for this to work is a fairly large catch, but being able to take your language learning course on the road is still incredibly useful if you're heading to foreign lands and want to brush up on your verbiage in transit. It works for all Rosetta Stone languages too, no matter which one you're learning!

Tapatalk HD

Price: £2.99 / $4.99
Developed By: Quoord Systems
App Purchases: No

We may be living in an age where we can save files virtually and control mobile phones with our voices, but good old internet forums are still very much alive and kicking. There's just something about having reasoned, lively or even downright heated conversations with many different people at once, available for everyone to read that just feels right, but having to jump from forum to forum to do that is a bit of a pain. If only there was a way of keeping all your favourite posting spots in the same place without much fuss...

Thankfully, Tapatalk does just that. The app enables you to you search the Internet for forums (either ones you're already a member of or new ones matching your interests), log in and keep them on an instant access list, letting you come and go as you please at the touch of an on-screen button. Managing accounts, viewing recent posts and then responding to them, sending private messages and viewing profiles – it's all easy to do. The only catch is that any forum you want to use needs to have the Tapatalk plug-in added to its back

end, but more and more are adding it every day. That means you're bound to find somewhere you can call a virtual home, packed with people to talk to... or argue with.

Skype

Price: Free
Developed By: Skype Software
App Purchases: No

Remember how we said that there were ways and means of getting around the fact that the iPad wasn't an iPhone so it couldn't make phone calls? Well, here's what we were talking about: the Skype app. Of course, the calls need to be between Skype users, but that's besides the point: it's free phone calls! And video calls too, even though Facetime has that covered. Either way, it's worth grabbing Skype purely to expand your communication options. Be warned, though, it needs a decent Wi-fi connection to work properly since Skype and 3G networks don't seem to play together very well. Still, when the cost of the call is free, who are we to argue?

Seesmic

Price: Free
Developed By: Seemsic Inc
App Purchases: Yes (remove ads)

Now that Facebook and Twitter are integrated with iOS 6, you might feel you don't need another app to manage your accounts. On the other hand, if you don't think much of the official apps for either social network, Seemic might be just what you're after. It lets you manage multiple Twitter and Facebook accounts and keeps everything neat and tidy for you, so you can always see what's going on. You can use all of the features you'd usually be able to access through the Facebook or Twitter apps, including adding photos or location info, and you'll get pop-up notifications when anyone tries to get in touch with you. If you really hate ad, it'll cost you £2.99 to get rid of them forever.

AIM (Free Edition)

Price: Free
Developed By: AOL Inc
App Purchases: No

Okay, so maybe you have SMS, Mail, Twitter, Facebook and all manner of other communication apps, but bar iMessage which is obviously limited to iOS-to-iOS messages only, can you instant message without it costing money? With AIM, you can. It's effectively the AOL equivalent of Microsoft's Windows Messenger (which there's also an app for, incidentally, so you might want to get that too if you already have an extensive network of contacts set up on your desktop computer), except you can set AIM up to connect with both Google Chat and Facebook Chat as well as using the AIM network. Think of it as the Swiss army knife of instant messaging apps (albeit one that's less pointy).

Your iPad mini And...
Navigation

The heightened (or shortened!) portability of the iPad mini means that it's a device far more likely to be taken around with you as you go about on your travels. And with its pretty much always-on web connection capability (particularly if you have a 3G/4G device), there's no reason you can't use it to help you make your way around, and put it to added good use!

Taking advantage of global satellite positioning technology (GPS), Apple has ensured that the iPad mini can be a location-centric piece of hardware. As such, you can then use a collection of apps to pinpoint your exact location. Using that, you can then, for example, find things of interest close to your geographic position.

Apple provides its own Maps application to deal with much of this, and we'll be taking you through the in and outs of that in this chapter. It has one or two problems (many still prefer Google Maps, which you can now access via the App Store), but it's still a good way to navigate around and to help you out when you're in a strange, unfamiliar place. The fact that Maps will orientate its display around which way you're pointing, for example, might just prove invaluable.

The GPS technology has another benefit as well. If you have an iPhone for instance, then you can use your iPad mini to help locate it, in case you happen to lose it! We'll be looking at how to do that, as well as exploring a further collection of apps, later in the chapter.

Finally, one word of note, which we've talked about before, but it's worth reiterating here. The downside of always-on web access, particularly 3G and 4G, is that it drains your battery and uses your data allowance up.

If you have constantly updated location data going to and from your iPad mini, that's bound to have an impact. On a long journey, then, at the very least, it's always worth making sure your iPad mini is fully charged. It's also worth being aware of just how much data you're using when you're on the move!

iPad mini

How To Use... Maps

Forget the folding-up nightmare that accompanies real paper maps. Apple Maps will give you step-by-step directions to anywhere you want to go, as well as offering all sorts of other location-specific useful info...

Step 1: Why Maps Matters

The Maps app comes pre-loaded onto your iPad as standard and can't be removed, so you might as well make use of it. It uses global satellite positioning technology, but loads the maps on the fly, so make sure that you have a 3G/4G or Wi-Fi connection available, otherwise it'll have trouble finding your location or calculating routes.

Step 2: Searching For Addresses

To find an address, tap the search bar to open the keyboard, then type in the address or name of the place you're looking for. Hit 'Search' and Maps will find it. To move around the map, simply tap and drag with your finger on the screen. If your contacts list has addresses as well as phone numbers in it, you can access and search for them by touching the blue book button in the top-left.

Step 3: Searching For Landmarks

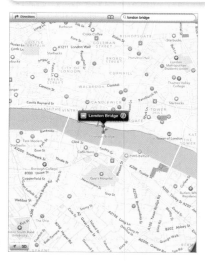

Maps can also find more than just fixed addresses. For instance, you can use it to look for famous landmarks or attractions – try entering things like 'Tower Of London' or 'London Bridge' for an example – or if you want to be more vague, you can search for general locations like towns, districts or cities just by entering the name and Maps will bring up a wide-area display.

Step 4: Searching For Services

Maps can even search for things like cinemas, restaurants or petrol stations. Just type what you need into the search bar and pins will appear showing nearby locations. You can then touch any pin for more information about it. This can be done either from your current location or from any location that appears after you type the address/postcode into the search bar.

iTip – FIND YOUR LOCATION
If you want to see where you are right now, press the small arrow button in the corner of the screen and, using 3G/4G/Wi-Fi coverage, Maps will find you immediately.

Step 5: Further Location Information

When displaying a precise location, Maps will display a small information panel for you. Pressing the blue arrow brings up information about the location if available, along with the option to get directions to or from that location. You can add information to your contacts by pressing 'Add To Contacts' or share the location via email, text message or Twitter.

Step 6: Zooming In

You can use the two-finger stretch/pinch gesture to zoom in/out of the map for a better view. To place a new location pin on the map, touch where you want it and hold your finger down until the new pin appears. You can then touch the blue arrow button in the information panel to add it to your contacts book, share it or calculate directions to/from it.

Step 7: Go 3-Dimensional

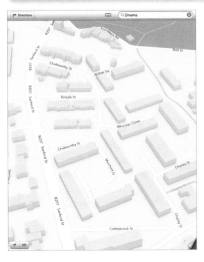

For a better idea of the lay of the land where you are, touch the 3D button in the bottom-left corner of the map. Apple Maps will add models of buildings to the map, and when you zoom in and out you can change angles. If you're lost, this might give you a better idea of where you are by helping you identify landmarks (and if not, it's still pretty interesting to look at).

Step 8: Traffic Overlays

If you touch the curled button in the corner of the screen, you'll reveal more view options. One worth having activated is the 'Traffic' setting, which provides a regularly updated view of how busy traffic is in your chosen location. If there's been an accident, Maps can get information on what's happened so you can make an informed decision about what to do next.

iPad mini

How To Use... Maps (continued)

Step 9: Hybrid Map Views

There are more options hidden under that curled up edge too for you to explore. By touching the Satellite option, for instance, you can switch from a map of the area to an actual photograph, which you can zoom in on just like the map. The Hybrid view gives you the best of both worlds by showing you an actual photograph but with street names labelled as well.

Step 10: Calculating Routes

Maps can easily calculate various routes between two different places. Just touch the Directions button at the top of the screen to bring up the 'Start' and 'End' bars. 'Start' will default to your current location but you can type an address, postcode or landmark in instead. You can also swap the 'Start' and 'End' bars by touching the wavy arrow button to reverse the route.

Step 11: Finding Alternative Routes

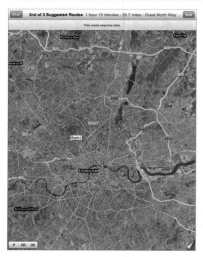

When you press the 'Route' button, Maps will calculate various routes to your destination. To cycle through the routes, just tap the labels. It picks car travel by default, but you can touch the buttons at the top to get the best on-foot and public transport routes too; tapping the clock button finds a suitable bus/train time, but this option isn't available in all regions.

Step 12: It's A Map, Not A Satnav

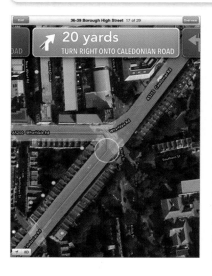

Unfortunately, the one thing lacking from Maps on the iPad is the hands-free feature you'd get with a satnav: it doesn't have a voice to bark orders at you with and you have to manually cycle through each directional step with the arrow buttons at the top. As a navigational tool, though – especially one used by a passenger or while on foot – Maps is still fantastic at getting you where you're going.

How To Use... Find My iPhone

In spite of its name, the Find My iPhone feature also works for iPads, and it means you'll never need to wonder where your iPad has disappeared to ever again

Step 1: Downloading Find My iPhone

The same app can be used to track all iOS devices, so go to the App Store and download Find My iPhone for free. If your device is lost or stolen, you can use another device to find it, make it emit an alarm or even remotely lock or wipe its contents. You can track your iOS device from any computer in the world by using either one of the MobileMe or iCloud services.

Step 2: Setting Up With iCloud

Now switch on the Find My iPhone settings: go into the Settings menu and click on the iCloud section. Make sure the 'Account' box at the top has your Apple ID inputted in it, then scroll down and hit the switch next to 'Find My iPhone' so that it says 'On'. You should also repeat this process with any other iOS devices that you happen to own.

Step 3: Find Yourself

Open the Find My iPhone app by touching the newly installed icon and sign in with your Apple ID and password. Your iPad will use GPS technology to figure out where it is, and display your current location on a map. It might not seem very useful now, since you already know where your iPad is - it's in your hands! - but this tracking ability could definitely come in handy at a later date...

Step 4: Find My iPhone On A Computer

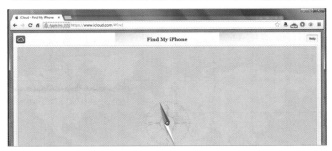

You can now track your iPad from any computer. Go to **www. icloud.com** then enter your Apple ID and choose 'Find My iPhone' to get an overhead view of your device's location (this will only work if your device is switched on and connected to a Wi-Fi network or has an active data connection.) If you need to, you can send a two-minute loud alarm and message of your choosing to your phone or even lock or wipe it remotely.

Related Navigation Apps

From satnavs to walking route guides, GPS locators to stargazing navigation, train times to finding a nearby restaurants, here are the best and most useful travel-based apps around…

TomTom for iOS

Price: £26.99 / $37.99
Developed By: TomTom
In-app Purchases: Yes (Voices and Maps)

If you'd like to transform your iPad into an in-car navigator, you'll need an app like this. It's similar to the software running in stand-alone TomTom units, and it uses GPS technology to figure out where you are and provide step-by-step info on where to get where you're going. You can only use this if you have a 3G enabled iPad, though, otherwise this app won't do you any good.

Where To Eat? Pro

Price: £0.69 / $0.99
Developed By: Networking 2.0
In-app Purchases: No

No matter where you are, you're going to need food at some point, but the thing you need to ask yourself is where to eat. Thankfully, that's the exact question that Where To Eat? HD answers, offering restaurants from around the world searchable by food type or location, a random shake selector if you can't decide and even detailed directions to whichever one you pick.

thetrainline

Price: Free
Developed By: thetrainline
In-app Purchases: No

Plan a rail journey and get up-to-the-minute info on live departures and arrivals with this app. You can save your journeys, find the fastest route to your destination and save a week's worth of journeys to view offline, but it's really the live travel info that's the selling point. It means if your train's delayed, you can head to the nearest Wi-Fi hotspot and still know exactly what's going on.

Plane Finder HD

Price: Free
Developed By: Pinkfroot Ltd
In-app Purchases: No

Just as there are apps for tracking cars and buses on the iPad, there's also one available for tracking planes – although that might not be useful if you're not already at an airport. Nevertheless, Plane Finder HD provides real-time 'virtual radar' information to show the same kind of air traffic maps that people in air traffic control towers would see, as well as enabling to you bookmark your favourite locations.

OutDoors GB

Price: £4.99 / $6.99
Developed By: RoadTour
In-app Purchases: Yes (more routes, maps)

Perfect for the outdoorsman in all of us (well, maybe not us: we prefer the indoors), this app shows every walking route across the whole of the UK using official Ordinance Survey maps. You get a 1:250k map included in the app, but can then get more at 1:50k and 1:25k as in-app purchases. Just make sure you get the right app: the one we're talking about has the words 'With National Parks' on the end of the title!

CycleMaps

Price: £1.49 / $1.99
Developed By: SZ Software
In-app Purchases: No

The bicycle equivalent of Navfree (reviewed on the right-hand page), since it uses the free OpenCycleMaps network to provide a complete listing of bike routes across the UK, allowing you to safely plan where you're going to go ahead of time. The app also includes plenty of options including saving routes and also a selection of routes for when you're outside the UK and looking to take a bit of a ride into the unknown.

Navfree GPS Live

Price: Free
Developed By: GeoLife
In-app Purchases: Yes (foreign maps, speed camera data, voices)

There are plenty of brand-name satnav apps available for Apple's iOS devices, but they cost an absolute fortune (for instance, the TomTom app is a whopping £49.99!). Navfree, on the other hand, is totally free, yet it works just as well as any big-name satnav, as well as offering a whole host of options to make it the perfect in-car app for those with a need for navigation.

Unlike big-name apps that use licensed Ordinance Survey data (which is why they're so expensive), Navfree makes use of OpenStreetMap, a user-editable map system that's been built up by over 35,000 people – think of it as the Wikipedia of map software. It's this system that helps keep Navfree free, although it does come with the caveat that some data may not be 100% accurate. Before you panic, though, we should say that we haven't found any problems with it during our extensive use of Navfree, and if you do come across an error, you can tell Geolife about the error using the app's built-in report tool or even go into OpenStreetMap and make the correction yourself.

Using Navfree couldn't be easier. You just enter a postcode, an address or even just touch a spot on the map and off you go – and as well as clearly spoken instructions, Navfree also comes with automatic rerouting if you miss a turn, a low-glare night mode, the ability to bookmark locations or listen to your iPad's music and much more. And did we mention it's free? Considering how much is crammed into it, that's the best bit. Don't forget the big catch, though: Navfree requires a 3G/4G signal to work, so it's not for those with Wi-Fi only iPads.

GoSkyWatch Planetarium

Price: £2.49 / $3.99
Developed By: GoSoftWorks
In-app Purchases: No

Now here's an interesting trick: why not try navigating by the stars! Stargazing apps are ten a-penny on the App Store (although they're mainly used for educational purposes, like the awesome Solar Walk), but GoSkyWatch is different in that it's not just there for reference; you can use it to accurately determine what stars are directly above and around you. Just point your iPad's camera into the sky and watch as the app maps out which star is which in real-time using augmented reality, or ask it where a certain planet is and marvel as it points you in the right direction. Not just one for budding astronomers, GoSkyWatch is genuinely impressive to see in action.

Find My Car For iPad

Price: £0.69 / $0.99
Developed By: Presselite
In-app Purchases: Yes (augmented reality)

The Find My iPhone of the motoring world, albeit one that requires a little more effort to function. You simply turn on the app when you park your car to set its location, then reactivate the app when you've forgotten where you put it to see it on a map. You can also take a picture and leave a note to better define where you parked or, if you pay 69p for the augmented reality add-on, see arrows projected on the ground in front of you through your iPad camera guiding you back. Just make sure you get the right Find My Car app, as there are several with the same name, but this is the best one! Remember though, it's only useful for iPads with 3G/4G connectivity.

Spyglass

Price: £2.49 / $3.99
Developed By: Pavel Ahafonau
In-app Purchases: No

One for the orienteering types among you, Spyglass takes the basic compass concept and turns it on its head by adding so many features you won't know where to start. From projecting accurate headings on a live camera image and having a sniper-style range finder built in, to providing a sextant, tactical military-style GPS, gyrocompass, inclinometer, maps and even augmented reality navigation highlighting positions of the sun, moon and nearby landmarks, it's every navigation tool in one with a few more thrown in for good measure. Considering the iPad lacks the Compass app of the iPhone, this might be an essential purchase for some people.

iPad mini

iPad mini

Uncooked Media Ltd, 3 East Avenue,
Bournemouth, Dorset, BH3 7BW
www.uncookedmedia.com
Telephone 01202 586035

Editorial
Simon Brew, David Crookes, Sarah Dobbs,
Anthony Enticknap, Martin Mathers

Design
Ian Feeney, Adrianna Haniff

Contributors
Jonny Austin, Mike O'Sullivan,
Chris Schilling, Geoff Spick.

Customer Services
08453 306540
customerservice@uncookedmedia.com

Editorial Director
Darren Herridge
wonderdaz@gmail.com

Finance Director
Tim Harris
tim@selectps.com

Printed by
Printed by Acorn Web Offset